NOT SHOOTING
and
NOT CRYING

Recent Titles in
Contributions in Military Studies

NOT SHOOTING

and

NOT CRYING

Psychological Inquiry into Moral Disobedience

RUTH LINN

Contributions in Military Studies, Number 85

GREENWOOD PRESS

NEW YORK • WESTPORT, CONNECTICUT • LONDON

Library of Congress Cataloging-in-Publication Data

Linn, Ruth.
   Not shooting and not crying : psychological inquiry into moral
disobedience / Ruth Linn.
      p. cm. — (Contributions in military studies, ISSN 0883–6884
; no. 85)
   Bibliography: p.
   Includes index.
   ISBN 0–313–26497–X (lib. bdg. : alk. paper)
   1. Conscientious objectors — Israel — Psychology.   2. Lebanon —
History — Israeli intervention, 1982-   –Conscientious objectors–
Israel.   I. Title.   II. Series.
UB342.I75L56   1989
355.2′24′095694 — dc19   88–24720

British Library Cataloguing in Publication Data is available.

Library of Congress Catalog Card Number: 88–24720
ISBN: 0–313–26497–X
ISSN: 0883–6884

First published in 1989

Greenwood Press, Inc.
88 Post Road West, Westport, Connecticut   06881

Printed in the United States of America

The paper used in this book complies with the
Permanent Paper Standard issued by the National
Information Standards Organization (Z39.48–1984).

10 9 8 7 6 5 4 3 2 1

Contents

Tables

Acknowledgment

This book is the joint effort of many dear people whom I want to thank. At the top of the list stand my three wonderful children — Yair, Gilat, and Erez (who was born two months after the war broke out). I thank my husband Shai, who served as a commander of a combat medical battalion in endless reserve service in Lebanon from the beginning of the war, for teaching me various facets of courage. The wounded Israeli soldiers and Arab civilians whom they rescued in several heroic missions in minefields and under fire probably share my gratitude, as well as my questions regarding the meaning of life and death, honesty, conscience, and morality in the real world.

Very special thanks goes to two figures of highly moral stature: Mrs. Sybil and Mr. Steven Stone, who have been and always will be advocates of justice and peace and who were among the few to foresee the present moral dilemmas long before we had the courage to examine them.

I am deeply indebted to Professor Perla Nesher, who supported my line of inquiry, as a friend and as a Dean of the School of Education, and who secured the first financial support for the study. I thank Professor Adir Cohen, the Head of the Education Department, Professor Miriam Ben Peretz, the Dean of the School of Education, and all my friends at the school of education for the unique way each of them supported me while I wrote this book.

The advice, friendship, and understanding of Mr. David Bukai, the Academic Secretary of Haifa University, was a very special source of encouragement and insight, without which this book could not have been written.

In writing this book, I was privileged to spend two exciting years as a visiting research associate at the Harvard Graduate School of Education with Professor Carol Gilligan and at Maryland University with Professors David and Mady Segal. I owe much to their scholarly skills and friendships.

I am grateful to my American friends who encouraged me at various stages of the study: Mrs. Shirly and Mr. Micky Blumfield, Ms. Lilly Rivlin, Mr. Jonathan Jaccoby, Professor Nancy and Steve Schlossberg, Professor Michael and Anne Noone, Professor Saul and Posey Rogolsky, Professor Peter and Abi Steinglass, Dr. John and Kathy Turke, Dr. Sandy Stanly, Ms. Gail Raanan, and Ms. Diane Diamond-Sternberg.

Special thanks goes to the Brecher family, the late Susan Brecher, Molly Brecher, and Rose Sidney, who were always hospitable and helpful. I have special, warm memories of the late Henry Peterson for his friendship, and dedicated love of Israel in good and bad times.

The final effort in writing this book was made possible by the support and encouragement of a dear and special friend, Ms. Cora Weiss, via the Rubin Foundation and the Funding Exchange. Without her help, the book could not have been published.

I thank Dr. James Sabin, the Executive Vice President of Greenwood Press, for his most considerate and constructive review of the book. I would also like to thank Ms. Aliza Brown, the Executive Secretary of the Research Authority and Mrs. Shoshana Zalka, who were always helpful with a smile.

Special thanks go to the Maimon and Linn families, Mr. Yaakov Khoushy for his unconditional love and support, and to Dr. Dan Khoushy who so generously guided my first steps in publication on moral development and in learning the secrets of the computer.

Finally, I would like to thank all the soldiers whom I quote in the book for their willingness to share with me their moral pain and their struggle to incorporate social criticism with committed citizenship.

Introduction

I belong to a special generation within the Israeli society — a generation that was born after the War of Independence and that grew up with their parents' hopes and illusions that there would be no more wars. This trend was strengthened by the decisive victory of the 1967 Six Day War. Since then, however, we have faced many bitter wars — each of them increasing the moral dilemmas we were asked to resolve: the War of Attrition (1967–1970), the 1973 Yom Kippur War, military campaigns against terrorists in between, the Litani operation (1978), the Lebanon war (1982–1985). While I am writing this (January 1988), we are fighting an undeclared war in the occupied territories.

As I grew up and personally served in the front line during the War of Attrition, I have come to realize the real life drama of war, a drama identical to that portrayed by the Hollywood filmmakers. A drama with one basic difference — in real war, there is no music . . .

But there are tears. Within Israeli society, the tears of soldiers became a famous landmark in its various wars — a landmark of its various moral dilemmas and resolutions. Starting from the 1967 war, there are the paratroopers who captured (or united) Jerusalem, and expressed their relief and astonishment by crying next to the Wailing Wall — the last remaining part of the Jewish Temple that was mainly destroyed by the Romans in 70 A.D., after which Jews were thrown out of their land.

Following the 1973 Yom Kippur War, Israeli troops were often sent to disperse youth demonstrations in the occupied territories, mainly with tear gas. Some Israeli soldiers found themselves obeying the orders but simultaneously resisting them. Literally they were *shooting and crying.*

The paratroopers found themselves crying again, this time during the war in Lebanon (1982–1985), when they were questioning the moral meaning of their prolonged stay and actions in the area. Many soldiers shared this cry, manifested their protest in different ways, but nevertheless continued fighting. Throughout the three years of war, about 150 soldiers chose to adopt an unconventional mode of moral resolution: they disobeyed the command to serve in Lebanon, and preferred to be sentenced and imprisoned. They argued that such service would violate their consciences.

At the present time, in addition to the turmoil in the territories, a young generation of paratroopers is fighting back the persistent attempts of various terrorists to infiltrate from the Lebanese border in order to capture civilians as hostages. When mourning over the losses of their friends in fighting, they are comforted by their general. "Only those who know how to cry now know how to fight. To cry as a sign of mourning over a friend who was killed is not a sign of weakness. It is a sign that though we have to be fighters, we remain human beings" (*Ma'ariv,* May 2, 1988).

There has been relatively little focus on the psychological way in which the individual Israeli life-long soldier constructs, solves, and copes with moral dilemmas. Following the 1967 war, kibbutz members who were officers and soldiers highlighted, in a book named *The Seventh Day — Soldiers Talk about the Six Day War* (1971), their moral dilemmas regarding their face-to-face encounter with the enemy. These dilemmas were characterized by a one-way solution — you may preserve your moral principles in the battlefield at the cost of your and/or your friend's life, this is the only way innocent people would not be harmed; an integral part of the highly respected moral tradition of the IDF "Purity of Arms" (*tohar haneshek* in Hebrew).

The war in Lebanon, for which no song was composed, marked a new era of moral dilemmas for the Israeli soldier, wrought even before he set foot on Lebanese soil.

The road to Lebanon passes by the famous statue of a lion at the historic site of Tel Hai, under which is written "It is good to die for our country."[1] The individual soldier who was called to fight in Lebanon often found himself challenging this norm when he asked himself: Why should I fight? Why is it good to die for my country?

These questions and moral dilemmas were not exclusive to those soldiers who decided to refuse. However, the mode of moral resolution adopted by this extreme group of individuals, that is, refusal, was not a path of behavior familiar to Israeli society and is known to be a deviant kind of behavior within any army or society. Even though this action is defined by the actor as a noble one, an action that has been dictated by personal conscience, not much is known about the nature of this decision-making process or about its moral meaning both to the actor and the audience.

This book attempts to discover:

1. Why this phenomenon of conscientious objection emerged so dramatically during the war in Lebanon.

2. The moral-psychological characteristics of those soldiers who chose this course of action.

3. The impact of this action on the soldiers and Israeli society at large.[2]

NOTES

1. This declaration is believed to have been uttered by Josef Trumpeldor at the moment of his death in battle at Tel Hai in 1920. Tel Hai (meaning "Hill of Life"), located near the present northern Israel town of Kiryat Shemona (which suffered severe PLO bombing prior to the Lebanon War), was established in 1917 by a handful of Jews who bought the small bindery there from its Arab owners. The area was under French military control at the time of Arab attack. Eight of the Jewish defenders, including their commander Trumpeldor, died after a heroic stand. Every year, on the eleventh day of the month of Adar, "Tel Hai Day," youth from all over the country make a pilgrimage to this site, which has come to symbolize the new spirit and valor of the modern Jew in fighting.

2. This book consists of the author's published papers prior to the uprising in the territories.

_____ *Chapter 1* _____

The Individual Conscience at War

SEARCH FOR A THEORETICAL FRAMEWORK

"All that the Lord hath spoken we will *do* and *hear*" (Exodus 24:7).

This unquestioning acceptance of the Ten Commandments by the people of Israel portrays the moral person as the one whose actions are guided by certain external standards of excellence. By preceding HEAR with DO, the people of Israel did not simply conform to a set of rules but indicated their willingness to transform "religious laws into personal commands of personal deity" (Loevinger, 1976, 277). But, did they, indeed, succeed in pursuing this goal?

In spite of their dramatic promise, the people of Israel found out that in real life practice, it is not as simple to follow hypothetical prescribed moral principles. Moses climbed Mount Sinai but did not return for forty days. When left alone without their leader, when the situation was ambiguous and all their familiar expectations collapsed and while still clinging to the habitual state of mind of slaves, their first action under the pressure of circumstances was an immoral one: the building of a false god, the Golden Calf.

In the light of this discrepancy between the manifestation of hypothetical (verbal) prediction of moral competence and its actual practice, the dramatic placement of the action *(do)* prior to the judgment *(hear)* is indeed quite puzzling. It was also a puzzle for biblical interpreters who questioned the psychological dynamics of the construction of another god in the light of the unique moral commitment to one God. They argued that in real life practice the moral decision maker is always heavily dependent upon contextual forces of time (historical time), place (existing authorities), and habit (the dominant personal tendencies). Personal freedom in judgment and action, they further suggested, might be obtained only in the case of total devotion to the Torah (Leibowitz, 1976).

Following the inquiry into the source of personal wisdom used by individuals in conflicting moral situations, the New Testament shifted the emphasis from external criteria to "intrinsically valuable" criteria held by the human being who "will develop his potential worth" if only given the opportunity (Hogan, et al., 1978, 14). This concept of the individual as a free actor, essentially capable of rising above the circumstances of his environment by his own virtue, represents a different ideological position: the view of the moral person as having free choice and freedom to shape his own salvation (Bem, 1970). Historically, this view became central to the doctrine of modern education up to Dewey, and today is expressed in Lawrence Kohlberg's theory of, and research on, moral development.

In line with Piaget's pioneering work on children's moral judgment (1932/1965), Kohlberg (1958) conceptualized morality as a mode of choice between conflicting rights. He viewed the way individuals understand, construct, and maintain a sense of moral meaning in their social world as a function of their justice structure or moral stage, or the logical considerations and justifications that ought to be taken into account when faced with any hypothetical dilemma.

Kohlberg argued that when faced with hypothetical moral dilemmas (situations which revolve around conflicting rights and duties), individuals tend to construct their moral choices and to ascribe meaning to their actions according to six distinct stages of moral reasoning (modes of prescriptive valuing of socially good and right).

Kohlberg (1976, 1982, 1984) conceptualized six age-related stages of moral reasoning that develop with time and experience. He argued that the stages represent a gradual increase of the internal moral capacity to the point where the person's judgment is freed from individual and societal constraints. The model entails the premise that a morally mature person would become autonomous in his functioning.

The stages represent three possible approaches to any moral dilemmas with respect to society's moral norms: preconventional (stages 1-2), conventional (stages 3-4), and postconventional (principled) perspectives (stages 5-6):

1. The heteronomous stage (punishment and obedience orientation): *right* is blind obedience to rules and authority, avoiding punishment and not doing physical harm.

2. The stage of individualism and instrumental purpose and exchange (instrumental relativist orientation): *right* is serving one's own or others' needs and making fair deals in terms of concrete exchange.

3. The stage of mutual interpersonal expectations, relationships, and interpersonal conformity ("good boy/nice girl" orientation): *right* is playing a good (nice) role, being concerned about other people and their feelings, keeping loyalty and trust with partners, and being motivated to follow rules and expectations.

4. The social system and conscience stage ("law and order" orientation): *right* is doing one's duty in society, upholding the social order, and the welfare of the society or group.

5. The stage of social contract or utility and of individual rights (social-contract legalistic orientation): *right* is upholding the basic rights, values, and legal contracts of a society, even when they conflict with the concrete rules and laws of a group.

6. The stage of universal ethical principles (universal ethical principle orientation): *right* means being guided by universal ethical principles that all humanity should follow (Locke, 1981, 168-169).

These stages determine actions by way of concrete definitions of rights and duties in a given situation. They are based on the premise that with an increase in the stage of moral development, the individual's judgment is more likely to be objective and fair since it is unaffected by personal and contextual constraints.

This abstract portrait of human functioning is obviously an ideal one. In real life practice, moral decisions are made in the context of specific moral problems and "must work in the context of the real life world" (Damon, 1983, 285). The highest stages in this "content free" structural system not only increase the likelihood of consistency in reasoning but are also expected to provide the morally "better" choices as leading inevitably to the valuing of human life: "one cannot follow moral principles (stages 5–6) if one does not understand and believe in them" (Kohlberg, 1976, 32). Thus, while Kohlberg provides no information as to whether a particular person will "live up to his stage of moral reasoning in a particular situation" (Kohlberg, 1976, 32), he considers the stages as powerful predictors of action, particularly with the advancing stages of moral development.

Kohlberg argues that there is a unitary developmental process in the course of both judgment and action development: "moral judgement development both causes moral action and arises out of moral action itself. A new moral judgement may guide new behavior while performance of new behavior may lead one to construct a new moral judgement" (Kohlberg, 1984, 506). Kohlberg believes that the moral stage development is a good predictor of the maturity of moral action. Yet, he acknowledges that the relations between the individual's hypothetical moral reasoning and his overt behavior are far from being fully unfolded: "From the point of view of cognitive developmental theory, the relation of the development of judgement to action is something to be studied and theoretically conceptualized" (Kohlberg, 1976, 46).

This book provides a unique opportunity for the examination of the complex path from the individual's judgment to action. This inquiry is focused on the experience of a unique group of moral actors: soldiers in the Israel Defense Forces (IDF), a group of individuals who claim that their action of refusing to perform reserve service on Lebanese soil during the war there, was constructed and executed by the dictate of their moral thinking.

The particularity of this mode of action to a given society seems to go far beyond the moral character of the actors. As suggested by Walzer (1970), conscientious objection is not the sole product of an individual's moral thinking, but rather a function of the character of the community, as well as the relations that exist between the two. On the rare occasions of analyzing soldiers' behavior during a war situation, Kohlberg indicates that in real life "the moral choice made by each individual soldier . . . [is] embedded in a larger institutional context of the army and decision making procedures. Their decisions are dependent in large part upon a collectively shared definition of the situation . . . in short the group 'moral atmosphere'" (Kohlberg, 1984, 571). When described independently from the context, an action of refusal to obey the law of military service, even if claimed to have been performed in the name of morality, should be regarded as primarily wrong. The context may present moral considerations that might override its apparent wrongfulness (Cohen, 1971). Chapters 1 and 2 portray the moral atmosphere within which the subjects in this study, Israeli reserve soldiers, experienced a clash between their conscientious claims and the demands of a state that professes to believe that it is fighting to protect social values and ideals (Scheissel, 1968).

Most often this clash is neither accidental nor irrational. Yet, particularly when their action involves disobedience to a legal law,[1] we cannot take for granted the individuals' claim that they are acting conscientiously, nor their sincere belief that what they do is right. Indeed, "While not claiming to be above the law or exempt from it, they do claim to be *right* in disobeying it in very special and perhaps even agonizing situations" (Cohen, 1971, 192), and therefore, rational extralegal reasonings for breaking the law showing that these nonlegal considerations override their obligation to obey, should be expected. In Kohlberg's terms, this claim for moral superiority (to be discussed in Chapter 3), is most likely to be heard from those individuals able to hold postconventional or principled moral perspectives. This mode of thinking entails the premise that when there is a conflict between the legal and moral domains, the moral should almost always take precedence because it represents the more objective and impartial solution within and across societies.

Limiting our inquiry to those individuals whose claims for moral superiority are bound to the secular sphere, two types of conscientious objectors might be found: one is the universal conscientious objector "who refuses registration and alternate service because he finds all cooperation with the military to be a compromise of his opposition to war" (Scheissel, 1968, 16). The other is the selective conscientious objector who claims to have the right to judge each war, the one who is willing to fight but insists on not fighting in a specific war which he may consider as holding unjust goals or being constructed unjustly, or both. In Kohlberg's terms the claim for moral consistency (to be discussed in Chapter 4) refers to cognitive structure rather than overt behavior. Principled objectors are more likely to manifest consistency in their hypothetical and actual mode of moral thinking. This search for consistency of justice structures is of particular interest in the case of the selective conscientious objector, whose overt moral conduct of resistance to the military service is not a way of life.

When a concrete action is at stake, the examination of "stage consistency" might be necessary, but it is not sufficient. There is a need to inquire whether there is a consistency between the actor's judgment concerning the morality of a given choice of action and the performance of the action: "personal consistency" or "integrity" (Blasi, 1983). In this way we can further learn why it was relevant for the actor to act in a certain way within a given situation, how the action contributed to the actor's sense of self consistency, and overall, why it was necessary for the actor to be involved with "both situation and action" (Blasi, 1983, 198). Operationally, it requires the examination of the specific moral choice (the content of moral judgment about the action) and why it was necessary to act upon it. The two types of moral consistencies are presented in Chapter 5, where the reasoning of soldiers who refuse to fight is contrasted with the reasoning of striking physicians.

Paradoxically, even when performed by a "majority of one," in Thoreau's words, a conscientious, deliberate, nonviolent public act of lawbreaking serves as a threat to the entire society and inevitably generates a primarily hostile response. Are there moral motives that might serve as a source of fear to the entire society? How do we identify them? An inquiry into these puzzles will be illustrated in Chapter 6, which examines the moral motivation of refusing soldiers who hold one of the most humane military roles: combat medics.

Particularly in times of war, the claim for moral superiority may create an a priori position of suspicion: is the refuser a loyal citizen? Or is he simply a coward hiding his fear with moral principles? How sincere is his moral pain? Can it be measured at all? Chapter 7 tackles this issue both from the point of view of the individual who strives to be believed as having acted conscientiously as well as from the perspective of those agents in society obliged to judge his conscientiousness.

Finally, the path from abstract moral understanding and morally meaningful performed action touches various intervening factors such as "moral atmosphere," "ego strength," (Kohlberg, 1984) or "responsibility" (Blasi, 1983). In the realm of concrete moral action, inquiry into the nature of the "nonmoral" factors that bridge judgment and action, becomes crucial for the understanding of judgment-action relationships and are discussed throughout the book but particularly in Chapters 4 and 5. Some "nonmoral" considerations, however, are extremely valuable if judged in terms of care considerations rather than on Kohlberg's justice scale (Gilligan, 1982a). Is the voice of justice the only moral voice heard by soldiers who refuse to obey orders for conscientious reasons? Chapter 8 is dedicated to this question.

Chapter 9 attempts to integrate those sociomoral factors that paved the way toward the conscientious refusal of fighting soldiers.

A comprehensive account of morality seems to require knowledge of both judgment and action, since "understanding guides the action and determines its specific meaning, while action brings moral understanding to its natural completion" (Blasi, 1983, 178). Empirically, it is recommended that the examination of the complex relations between judgment and action would start from the individual's concrete behavioral choice (Blasi, 1983).

This book begins with a concrete and dramatic behavioral choice within Israeli society: the refusal of reserve soldiers to fulfill one of their most serious obligations as citizens, that is, to fight for their own state (Walzer, 1970). The study began in September 1983, more than a year after the war broke out. It included thirty-six male subjects, randomly selected from a total of eighty-six reserve soldiers then serving prison terms for having refused to serve in Lebanon up to that date.

Each refuser (the individuals are regarded as refusers until their motivations are fully discussed) was interviewed individually at his home upon his release from prison. The interview lasted from between two to four hours and was taperecorded with the refuser's permission. It consisted of two parts. In the first part, the subject's stage of moral development was assessed, utilizing Kohlberg's (1984) first two dilemmas on Form B of the Standard Moral Judgment Interview (MJI) (see Appendix 1). The second part consisted of a semiclinical, open-ended interview aiming to identify each subject's Actual Moral Reasoning (AMR) in support of his action (see Appendix 2). The order of the two parts of the interview was altered between subjects.

The protocols were scored blindly by a qualified rater who had not done the initial interviewing and who was not aware of the subjects' identity. In line with Kohlberg's revised manual (Colby, et al., 1987), the scoring procedure involved the classifying of stage scores for each match between a manual criterion judgment and the moral judgment in the interview. The scores for the MJI and the AMR were given in the form of moral maturity scores as well as global scores. The moral maturity scores represent a weighted average of the issue scores and ranged from 100 (pure stage 1) to 500 (pure stage 5). Stage 6 does not appear in the revised scoring manual since in practice there is no difference between stages 5 and 6 (Gibbs, et al., 1982). The global score consists of a pure stage (the subject's modal level) or the transitional score (e.g., 3/4) when two stages are assigned an equal number of points. The AMR score was assessed clinically against Kohlberg's manual (see Appendix 3). Any conclusion at this stage of analysis is limited to this group.

The uniqueness of the study lies in its being the only moral/psychological investigation that has been conducted in Israel on this group of unknown reserve soldiers who conscientiously refused to fulfill their military obligation in Lebanon. It attempts to contribute to the field of moral psychology in two ways. First, it investigates an action of moral disobedience in an irreversible real life event that involved concrete life and death implications (Gilligan, 1982b). Second, it sharpens our understanding of moral disobedience in a social institution where discipline and obedience are fundamental prerequisites.

THE OBLIGATION TO FIGHT:
WHERE IS THE DILEMMA?

One of the most serious and critical moral obligations that a citizen may face at one time or another in life is the duty to fight (kill or be killed) for one's country (Walzer, 1970, 1977). For the Israeli male citizen, this is a life-long duty due to the unique system of the Israel Defense Forces. Israel's security is maintained largely by civilians in uniforms. Upon the completion of three years of compulsory service (starting at the age of eighteen) Israeli male citizens (Jewish and Druze) are required to perform one month of reserve service annually up to the age of fifty-five. Often, due to immediate threats from neighboring countries, the nature and the length of the service occurs on a war-time footing.

Since its establishment in 1948, the state of Israel with its four million citizens has had a continuous struggle for physical survival as it is surrounded by over one hundred million hostile Arab neighbors (with the exception of Egypt due to the recent peace treaty). The Lebanon war (1982–1985) was the sixth war this country had experienced during its short time of existence. It was preceded by the War of Independence (1948, with all the Arab countries), the Sinai campaign (1956, with Egypt), the Six Day War (1967, with Egypt, Syria, and Jordan), the War of Attrition (1967–1970, with Egypt), and the Yom Kippur War (1973, with Egypt and Syria).

In addition to these "conventional wars," Israel knew continuous attacks by terrorists from the very first day of its existence. Up to the 1956 war, Israel faced recurrent attacks by "Fedayeen" (self-sacrificers), who infiltrated from the Egyptian and Jordanian borders into Israeli settlements killing citizens in sudden attacks. Following the 1956 Sinai campaign, the Fedayeen attacks stopped, but were resumed in 1965 (largely without the support of the Arab countries). These attacks were escalated during the 1970s, mainly by the Palestine Liberation Organization (PLO), which was forcefully expelled from Jordan where it disrupted civilian life and threatened government stability (Merari, 1985). When denied permanent settlement and independent action by Syria, the PLO infiltrated the state of Lebanon, which has a long border along the northern region of Israel, the Galilee. Southern Lebanon became the PLO stronghold as well as one of the central bases for training international terrorists.

It is important to note that occasionally the PLO and other groups give the appearance of aspiring to regular counterforce military capability. However, their tactics and actions suggest they rely on terrorism (O'Brien, 1986). The following are some examples of the numerous terrorist attacks on Israel.

- On May 20, 1970, nine pupils and three teachers from a village in the Galilee (Avivim) were killed and nineteen other children wounded, when their bus was attacked by bazookas from an ambush.
- On May 30, 1972, twenty-six civilians were killed and seventy-six wounded at Ben Gurion Airport by three Japanese terrorists operating on behalf of the Popular Front for the Liberation of Palestine (PFLP).
- On June 5, 1972, eleven sportsmen from the Israeli Olympic delegation were massacred in Munich, West Germany.
- On May 15, 1974, twenty-four elementary school children were murdered and sixty-two others were wounded in a school in the Galilee town of Ma'alot by PLO terrorists demanding the release of Arab prisoners. After this experience, the IDF became more active in initiating rescue missions even in desperate situations.
- On June 28, 1976, an Air France plane that left Israel was hijacked by two PLO terrorists and two German terrorists and 105 Jewish and Israeli passengers were held hostage in Uganda, Africa. In a dramatic operation, the IDF succeeded in rescuing the hostages without harming the native civilian population.

The accumulation of terrorist attacks on civilians within the country reached a peak on March 11, 1978, when two public buses were hijacked near Tel Aviv, killing thirty-three people and wounding eighty-two. A week after this attack, the IDF launched an attack upon Lebanon to destroy the PLO bases. This limited operation, named after the small river that marked the boundary of the territory attacked, the Litani, did not bring an end to the terror. In 1980, for example, terrorists entered a nursery in a kibbutz near the Lebanese border (Misgav Am) and took the babies as hostages. When the IDF struck back, the terrorists were killed, as well as one child.

These examples do not include the numerous bomb explosions within various Israeli cities and the continuous attacks with Russian Katyusha missiles on Israeli cities and settlements in the Galilee from the PLO bases located a few miles from this region. These bombings from Lebanon reached a peak in the summer of 1981, when thirty-three settlements were bombed at the same time for ten days and many citizens in the Galilee decided to leave their homes (Gal, 1986).

Until this hot summer, Israel had not declared an all-out offensive against the terrorists but chose rather to retaliate after certain attacks or to initiate small, limited, preventive operations. None of these tactics seemed to prevent terrorist attacks in the country or against its citizens outside the country. However, after the 1981 attacks, some were considering the possibility of an all-out military campaign in order to prevent further escalation of the terrorists' attacks.

Can we expect an a priori moral dilemma when the individual soldier is called to fight an initiative war against terror vis-à-vis a retaliatory one? Can we expect any change in his motivation to fight?

TYPE OF WAR AND THE SOLDIER'S MORAL DILEMMA

There are two ways in which war can, and should, be morally judged: first, in regard to the justice of the war objectives (*jus ad bellum*) and second in regard to the conduct of the war (*jus in bello*). A war is just if it is aimed at protecting fundamental values such as national independence, communal freedom and the lives of people, when all other means of protecting them are not sufficient (Walzer, 1977). Justice in war refers mainly to the discrimination between combatant and noncombatant and the prevention of unnecessary damage.

Walzer argues that *jus ad bellum* and *jus in bello* are "logically independent." "It is perfectly possible for a just war to be fought unjustly and for an unjust war to be fought in strict accordance with the rules" (1977, 21). Though, theoretically, these sets of judgments are independent, "the dualism of *jus ad bellum* and *jus in bello* is at the heart of all that is most problematic in the moral reality of war" (Walzer, 1977, 38).

These rules of war consist of "two clusters of prohibitions attached to the central principle that soldiers have an equal right to kill. The first cluster specifies when and how they can kill, the second whom they can kill" (Walzer, 1977, 41). The distinction between *jus ad bellum* and *jus in bello* is important since "we draw a line between the war itself, for which soldiers are not responsible, and the conduct of the war, for which they are responsible, at least within their own sphere of activity" (Walzer, 1977, 38). On the practical level, the soldier's main concern is the second set of rules:

"How those victims of war who can be attacked and killed are to be distinguished from those who cannot" (41).

While the application of moral rules of war is not a simple task for the individual soldier, it is much harder when these rules are not observed by the enemy, as in terrorist warfare. Terrorism is a mode of fighting that has probably characterized modern civilization from its inception (Sandler, et al., 1983). The vulnerability of democratic societies to terrorist activities is very similar to the one experienced by various states in the past (Rappoport, 1984). Terrorism today, however, seems to differ from earlier forms in its frequency and in the extent of its violence (Netanyahu, 1986).

In its most common definition, the word "terrorism" is often used to describe revolutionary violence. The method of terrorism is its random capturing of innocent people, where the victims would "feel themselves fatally exposed and demand that their government negotiate for their safety" (Walzer, 1977, 194).

Most of the researchers in the field of terrorism tend to share the idea that "the only norm of terrorism is effectiveness in terrorizing" (O'Brien, 1986, 154). Following O'Brien, the random attack on individuals and representatives of the country aims to leave the message that "no one is safe." These attacks are followed either by the demand for ransom, release of political prisoners, economic succession, or the acceptance of a utopian revolutionary agenda. Whereas the last demand might be an unacceptable ultimatum, the other demands are sometimes accepted by leaders of democratic countries, and eventually bring about future terrorist attacks.

The term terrorism has no precise or widely accepted definition. The difficulty in defining it has led to the cliché: "One man's terrorist is another's freedom fighter." Its frequent use may suggest that when no objective definition of terrorism is constructed, there can be no universal standards of conduct in peace and war (Jenkins, 1986). At a 1979 international conference in Jerusalem, terrorism was defined as "the deliberate and systematic murder, maiming, and menacing of the innocent to inspire fear for political ends" (Netanyahu, 1986, 9). In fact, the terrorists' strategy might be part of conventional war, or guerilla war (Walzer, 1977, 38). Yet, it represents a different moral position in regard to the moral laws of war accepted by society.

Compared with terrorism, conventional war has clear norms:

there is a neutral territory that is recognized by the fighting forces, the armed forces are identified, there is a restriction to certain arms in the battlefield, and there is an awareness that the use of armed forces against civilians is exceptional or aberrational. In contrast, terrorism is aimed at the destruction of established norms (Laqueur, 1977). Unlike guerilla fighters who are not breaking the laws of war, who know who their enemy is and attack only superior combatants, terrorists blur the combatant-noncombatant distinction by saying that "WAR IS WAR and any attempt to define ethical limits to war is futile" (Netanyahu, 1986, 10).

When no distinction is made between combatant and noncombatant, nor in regard to the proportion of damage done, terrorism takes the entire free society as its field of combat, though, paradoxically, it very often demands the same treatment given to legitimate warfare. Thus when we abandon the cliché that one person's terrorist is another's freedom fighter, we can better understand (or adopt) Jenkin's definition that "One man's terrorist is everyone's terrorist" (1968, 9). The moral distinction between conventional warfare and terrorism is important not only for the understanding of the phenomenon of terrorism per se, but for the understanding of our moral right to fight it and what might motivate those who are obliged by society to do so to refuse.

According to O'Brien (1986), counter terrorist activities can be passive or active. Passive means concern the strengthening of society's internal security and so on, none of which raises fundamental moral dilemmas. Moral tension within a given victimized society and its army is more likely to occur when active means are proposed and executed. O'Brien delineates two modes of active responses to terrorism that are often used by the victimized society (particularly terrorism emanating from foreign countries): retaliation or preventive campaign. Table 1.1 presents the differences between the two types of counterattacks.

In the IDF tradition, a "preemptive strike" may be justified only when a war has already been initiated against Israel and therefore Israel reacts to an Arab change in the status quo. A "preventive campaign" should be initiated out of the assessment that otherwise there will be a change for the worse in the status quo. This type of logic is morally and legitimately questionable within the IDF tradition (Peri, 1983). Moreover, when terrorists are the target of

Table 1.1
Types of Military Response to Terrorism

Retaliation	Preventive
1. Following terrorist attack and is linked implicitly or explicitly to the terrorists' action.	1. True preemption of terrorists is conceivable but unlikely.
2. The rationale is punishment - the infliction of retribution on the terrorists and their supporters.	2. Inflicting serious long term damage on the terrorist and infrastructures.
3. Serves to satisfy an outraged society 's demand for retaliation and tends to reassure domestic opinion.	3. Might raise criticism within society.
4. Easier to justify legally and morally when linked to previous terrorist acts, than preventive measures against terrorists.	4. Hard to justify
5. Seldom provides sufficient answer to terrorism	5. Might become a source of deterrence to the terrorists
6. Leaves the initiative to the hand of the terrorists who can always reduce the pace and intensity of the hostile interaction if things seem to be going against them.	6. Aims to control the initiative of the terrorists and make them defensive

Source: O'Brien 1986, 156–157.

such military action, the conduct of the war might be problematic for the individual soldier who would be responsible and would have to justify his action (Walzer, 1977).[2] Thus, for example, when terrorists' military positions, like those of the PLO, are located within schools, hospitals, and civilian settings, it imposes an a priori moral dilemma for the IDF soldiers holding the ethical code of purity of arms or *tohar haneshek* in Hebrew.

This concept, as explained by Gal (1986), evolved during the prestate clashes with the Arabs. It refers basically to the idea of keeping the weapon "pure" by preserving its use for definite cases of self-defense. In its broad sense it implies the preservation of "humanistic norms in combat, refraining from unnecessary bloodshed, and avoiding, at all cost, harming civilians in general and women and children in particular. It further means avoiding damage to sacred buildings, treating POWs in a humane way and totally refraining from looting, raping and other atrocities" (Gal, 1986, 239).

The translation of this ideal moral code into practice manifested itself in two ways. First, before sending their soldiers into the battlefield or any military mission, the IDF commanders are taught not to expect blind obedience and to provide the soldiers with the moral logic of their assigned mission. Second, the IDF commanders traditionally adopt a "follow me" policy: by leading their soldiers, the commanders not only set an example of courage and bravery, but they practice their proclaimed moral responsibility. This tradition is responsible for the high toll of casualties among the IDF commanders throughout the Israeli wars. With the Israeli traditional logistics of "few against many," these concepts of "purity of arms" and "follow me" brought about extra casualties among the Israelis, but was nevertheless regarded by army officers as one of the solid sources of strength of the IDF. As stated by Colonel (Res.) Meir Pa'il: "Purity of arms does not detract in the least from the fighting ability of our soldiers" (Hardan, 1985).

In the Lebanon war, where battles against the PLO were fought in heavily populated civilian areas, this faith seems to reach a new apex. Though the IDF soldiers were strictly instructed to observe the above guidelines, mainly not to harm innocent civilians, its translation into practice revealed itself in some forms of motivational crisis, as the following chapters illustrate.

NOTES

1. Cohen (1971) would probably refer to the subjects of this study as civil disobediants. In his opinion, "The conscientious objector — whether or not he is right in his repugnance for all military activity — acts entirely within the provisions of the law." Conscientious objection, in the normal sense, may be considered as a form of protest, but it is never disobedient (p. 42). In this book, I refer to the subjects as "refusers" (or, alternatively, as selective conscientious objectors) in order to contrast them with *conscientious objectors* in Israel, a status given only to religious Jews.

2. Can we expect any difference in soldiers' motivation when called to fight terror vis-à-vis conventional war? Is there a difference in the motivation of soldiers in a victimized society when called to fight terrorists in a preventive or a retaliatory attack? On the one hand, it may be argued

that soldiers would be more motivated to fight terrorism rather than a conventional war for the following reasons:

1) Actions of terrorism cross the boundaries between being a soldier and a citizen. Since "no one is safe," the individual soldier can easily visualize a possibility where he and his family might become a target of terrorist actions.
2) Due to the coverage of the media and the consequent dramatization of the terrorists' brutality, the war against terrorists might be perceived by the soldier as more immediate (remove the daily threat) and concrete (as he is able to personalize the enemy) than in the case of a conventional war fought against an unknown army (which might be a group of innocent people).
3) In the fight against terror, the soldier is called upon to kill the one who has already performed a killing himself, a fact that may morally legitimize the fighting.

Alternately, it might be argued that these facts might lower the soldier's motivation to fight terror:

1) The fight against terror is primarily the fight *among* or even sometimes *against* civilians. This "battlefield" raises an a priori moral dilemma in regard to the killing of innocent civilians for any professional soldier, but even more so for a civilian reservist.
2) Unlike a conventional enemy army, the terrorists have more access to the mind of the citizens due to the media coverage. Thus, in a case where terrorists claim to believe in some noble cause behind their action (even though they might have other means to achieve it), it might appeal to the soldier who favors certain political or moral solutions (as a civilian).
3) One of the few "privileges" soldiers have in war, is the knowledge of "who is my enemy." In the fight against terror, this privilege is not always there.

Chapter 2

The Israeli Soldier as a Selective Conscientious Objector: Why during the War in Lebanon?

Conscientious objection to war may be defined as a refusal to participate in a military mission in order to protect one's own moral integrity, and/or effect change in society. It is very often referred to as civil disobedience. It is known to be a purely personal, moral action, "which is sometimes the only resort of the principled but lonely man" (Walzer, 1968, 14). Both modes of objection, however, are generally unfamiliar to the Israeli public. From a societal point of view, nonreligious objection to war out of personal and ethical principles lacks legal status in Israel (Glazer and Glazer, 1977). In spite of the five frequent and bitter wars this country has experienced since its establishment in 1948, conscientious objection has been very rare, consisting of a few individuals whose sporadic challenges to military service have hardly reached public attention (Blatt, et al., 1975).

On three occasions (1970, 1978, and 1987), but most dramatically in 1970, groups of high-school graduates sent letters to the minister of defense indicating their intention of refusing to be drafted and particularly to serve in the occupied territories. The most famous among them was a soldier named Gad Elgazi who, even as a school boy, had refused to go on day trips across the Green Line (the pre-1967 borders of Israel). After his conscription, he served with distinction in his unit until he was ordered to serve with the unit across the Green Line. He refused on five separate occasions to obey the order, for which he was punished with a total of 120 days in the camp lockup. When he again refused to obey orders, he was given a full court martial in January, 1981, and was sentenced to a year in prison (and eventually spent nine months in a military prison). The prosecutor in the case said in his summation that the army would not be able to function if every soldier were free to act according to his conscience, however exalted his beliefs. On the contrary, highly moral soldiers like Elgazi were badly needed in problematic areas such as the occupied territories. However, the fact that Elgazi's parents were active members of Rakach (the communist and anti-Zionist political party) enabled many to dismiss his action as a model of a conscientious or selective conscientious objector.

Obviously, a few cases of resistance to military service were insignificant when considering the uniqueness of military service in Israel. In times of war, this country can mobilize the largest army in the world in proportion to its population, composed mainly of civilian reservists. In spite of the continuous interruption of the individual's civilian life by the annual routine reserve duty, and unexpected long-term service in crisis situations, the motivation to serve the country is widespread. As noted by Gal (1986), until the war in Lebanon "the IDF soldier knew exactly why he was serving and what he was fighting for. Military service was an obvious need resulting from the surrounding threats" (247).

In the reality of few against many, the motivation of the individual soldier makes the quality of the army. According to a former IDF general:

This quality consists of . . . motivation, the reserve army and technology. The most important is the motivation. For this to exist, there should be a feeling and awareness of unity of fate. But this is not enough. It should be followed with a unity of goal, national consensus. Only on this ground can individual and collective motivation emerge. People in a democratic country will hardly be ready to sacrifice their lives for wars that are not related to their existence. . . . The reserve makes the quantity of the Israeli army, but (even) more . . . its quality . . . which consists of obligation on the individual level. [*Ha'aretz*, October 10, 1984]

The war in Lebanon (June 1982 to June 1985) seems to have put an end to this smooth functioning of the Israel Defense Forces. On June 6, 1982, following an attempted assassination of the Israeli ambassador in England, the IDF opened the "Peace of the Galilee" campaign, aimed at invading Southern Lebanon to a distance of forty kilometers from Israel's northern border in order to destroy the Palestine Liberation Organization in this territory, from which numerous terrorist attacks had originated. What was announced and expected to be a forty-eight- to seventy-two-hour operation against the PLO's infrastructure across the Galilee frontier expanded far beyond its original scope. "Peace of the Galilee" could have been perceived as a just military mission if performed as a limited operation. Officially the war lasted till June 11, 1982, and at least in this period of time, was backed by relative national consensus. Since then, however, the fighting continued between numerous ceasefires. This expanding and prolonged military mission seemed to deviate from the strict notion of "no choice" wars to which the Israelis were accustomed over the years.

The expansion of the war against the PLO and its allies and against the Syrian army (until the PLO was evacuated from Beirut in September 1982) provoked a growing debate in Israel regarding the justice of the war and the possibility of maintaining justice in the war. With the army staying in Lebanon beyond this date, gradually waging a continuous battle against the guerrillas in this area, the most common reference to the conflict was the "Lebanon war." For three years, the Israeli civilians were called to perform reserve service on Lebanese soil. With the increasing resistance of the native population in Lebanon, this service very often involved military clashes and ambushes, some of which were more severe than those occurring during the war. For the purpose of further analysis of the phenomenon, it is important for the reader to retain the distinction between the "war period" and the "occupation period" following September 1982.

Beyond the unexpected and proportionately large number of casualties (654 dead, 3,859 wounded, 4 missing in action, and 15 hostages) (Israel TV April 30, 1985), about 150 reserve soldiers refused to join their units in their assigned military mission in Lebanon. (The total number of 150 does not include the potential refusers, whose requests not to serve in Lebanon were granted by their immediate, sympathetic commanders.) The first cases of refusal became known to the public on September 22, 1982, following the quasi victory of war and the evacuation of the PLO terrorists from Beirut. An IDF spokesman announced that morning that three reserve soldiers had been tried for refusing to serve in Lebanon for moral reasons. In the following months, there were three refusals per month on average, reaching a peak in one month (May 1983) of twenty-seven refusers (this number seems to be related to the escalation of the anti-IDF terrorism in Lebanon: in this month there were one hundred severe incidents that left nine soldiers dead and twelve wounded). The IDF authorities treated the refusals as a discipline problem: because they refused to obey the order to join their unit, they were sentenced to jail for from fourteen to thirty-five days (which is the maximum number of days of imprisonment for this type of offense). About fifteen of them went to jail two and three times throughout the entire war when facing additional drafts. Most of the soldiers who objected to the war chose to fulfill their duty. Upon the return of the reservists from service, many took off their uniforms and went out to demonstrate against the war, as civilians, in front of the government offices.

The Israeli public did not know how to approach this new phenomenon. This is "a new melody within the Israeli society" the press was quick to announce (*Ha'ir,* March 11, 1983). The refusing soldiers were named *sarvanim* (meaning refusers in Hebrew), a name which emphasizes the obligation they were not fulfilling without any reference to the possible moral concerns they might have held. In spite of the growing public controversy over the war (with the prolonged stay on Lebanese soil), the *sarvanim* were condemned almost unanimously as leftists, delinquents, and lawbreakers who were undermining democracy (*Ha'aretz,* October 3, 1983). Social researchers as well seem to have been influenced by the hostile atmosphere revolving about the refusers. So it is not surprising that the author had severe difficulties independently obtaining names of refusers in order to study the moral nature of their claims. The uniform response to inquiries regarding their identity was "I have no friends like that."

The particularity of this phenomenon to the Lebanon war suggests that a comprehensive understanding of it requires primarily an inquiry beyond the nature of the refusers' moral character. As suggested by Walzer (1970), conscientious objection is not solely the product of an individual's moral thinking, but rather a function of the character of the community, as well as the relations that exist between them. Which contextual factors enabled these soldiers to challenge one of the most serious obligations as citizens, to fight for their own state (Walzer 1970)?

BACKGROUND OF THE REFUSERS

Thirty-six subjects were randomly selected from a list of eighty-six reserve soldiers who had been in jail up to this date as a consequence of their refusal to serve in Lebanon. Their ages ranged from twenty-three to forty-six years (mean 31.1, mode 28), and they came from the three main cities in Israel and five kibbutzim. Thirty-four subjects had European backgrounds (Ashkenazi). Sixteen were married (eleven with children), five were divorced (four with children), and fifteen were single. Twenty-three had academic degrees including four PhDs and three were doctoral candidates (mean 14.9 years of study). One subject was a captain, four were lieutenants, two were second lieutenants, seventeen were sergeants, and the remainder corporals and below. They were attached to paratroop, infantry, engineering, artillery, armored, and medical units. In terms of military role, medics made up the largest homogeneous group (seven). Twenty-two had military experience in war prior to this conflict. Twenty-four had previously served in the occupied territories. Twenty-six subjects decided to refuse *after* serving in Lebanon. Thirty subjects were the only refusers in their unit. Twenty-eight subjects did not make any attempt to convince others. Thirty subjects asked to return to their unit upon their release from prison. Five subjects were at the same site — Ansar — prior to their refusal. In terms of political orientation, three defined themselves as Communists, eighteen as Zionist leftists, and fifteen as close to the orientation of the Labor party.

The demographic data of this study suggest that the typical Israeli soldier refusing to serve in Lebanon can be portrayed as an experienced reserve soldier in his thirties (and when over thirty, typically married with children) and an Ashkenazi college graduate who served in the Lebanon war prior to his decision to refuse out of what he defined as serious moral concerns. These data provide some benchmarks for further inquiry as to the particularity of the phenomenon to this war:

1.   Objection to This Specific War

These soldiers seem to be selective conscientious objectors: those who object to the use of military power as a right rather than as a duty (Melzer 1975). The data suggest they did not object to serving before the Lebanon war. On the contrary, twenty-two subjects (61 percent) were full participants in previous military missions. Those who were not included in this category were either too young to serve or belonged to units that did not take part in these missions. Why, then, did these soldiers object to this war?

2.   The Moral Reality of the War

The data show that twenty-six subjects (72 percent) decided to refuse after serving in the Lebanon area, either during the war (nineteen subjects) or during reserve service following this period (seven subjects). Due to the guerilla fighting in Lebanon, service in the reserves following the war was very often more dangerous than the initial phase of the war. What particular experiences during the war led them to choose this mode of moral objection?

3.   Occupied Territories

Twenty-four subjects (68 percent) served in the occupied territories prior to their Lebanon experience. What role did that duty play in their decision to refuse?

4.   Moral Atmosphere of Protest

"In order to disobey," said Fromm, "one must have the courage to be alone." (Fromm, 1981, 21). Indeed, thirty subjects (83 percent) were the only refusers in their unit. Twenty-eight (78 percent) indicated that they did not even try to convince other soldiers to do the same. Given the fact that this deviant behavior exposes the individual to various social pressures, such as an attack upon his character, damage to his reputation, and being regarded as unpatriotic (Cohen 1971), it is important to examine the moral atmosphere that enabled the refuser to individually bridge the chasm between his judgment and action.

5. Ansar: The Final Straw

Five subjects decided to refuse after serving at one specific site: Ansar, a prisoner camp in Lebanon for the PLO terrorists. In their interviews, many who did not serve there, as well as those who did, referred to the camp as violating their moral boundaries. What made this place a practical and symbolic final straw?

WHY DID THE SOLDIERS REFUSE?

1. Objection to this Specific War

As noted before, there are two ways in which war can be judged: first, in regard to the objectives and reasons of the countries involved (*jus ad bellum*), and second, in regard to the means taken by the fighters (*jus in bello*). As for the first judgment, the most prevalent definition of a "just war" is one that aims at the nation's self-defense. Traditionally, there was no discrepancy between the title of the Israeli Army — the Israel Defense Forces — and its function of protecting national security (Luttwak and Horowitz 1983). The Lebanon war seemed to deviate from the conventional definition of a defensive war.

It was started as a preventative war, based on the assumption, or rather estimation, that in the near future there would be a kind of deterioration in the status quo between the PLO and Israel. In spite of the different nature of the war, the reserve soldiers' dedication and courage under fire were taken for granted. The traditional "no choice" secret weapon of the Israeli soldiers in the familiar situation of few against many seems to have been lacking in this definition of war. On the individual's part, the unfortunate readiness for self-sacrifice was substituted by the profound dilemma: Why should I fight?

This dilemma was not exclusive to the refusers in this study, but rather was shared by other reserve soldiers who objected to the war yet condemned refusal as the wrong solution. The following quoted from a speech by a spokesman of the Peace Now movement (see p. 36) illustrates this line:

The Lebanon war is primarily a war . . . in which people had no faith . . . even from the outset. This is the first time the Israeli soldier had been obliged to find within himself the willingness to fight and be killed in a nondefensive war. This is the first time that the question "where is the limit?" has so vividly been raised (*Ha'aretz,* September 23, 1983).

Though asking themselves at the onset of war, "Why should I fight?" none of the soldiers in this sample dared consider refusal at first. Said one:

My decision not to refuse on the first day of the war needs to be analyzed in the right context. . . . You are called in the middle of the night, the atmosphere is of blood, fire, and casualties . . . combined with some kind of pressure, anxiety and fear . . . you are all alone to make the decision. All that you know at this moment is that the country may have been attacked by its hostile neighbors and that it is your responsibility as a citizen to give all that you can in such a crisis . . . and if there is a real need for a military operation you want to do a good job . . . I also understand that a soldier cannot be informed of all the details of certain situations . . . and there is also a fear of the extreme reaction of the army if you refuse at this moment . . . ; and you want to believe that all the values of the Israel Defense Forces are still intact.

This confidence in the moral values of the IDF gradually diminished as the war became prolonged and went beyond the obvious notion of a just war as being primarily a limited one (Walzer, 1977). Another soldier related:

I understand that there is no opportunity to inform each soldier of the threat facing the nation and that for security reasons, no information could be given. Although the feeling of uneasiness was with me from the first day, it was only later, as the war continued, that my frustration reached its peak. I expected that with the ending of the war, the government, being democratic, would come and say, "Well, we could not inform you before about the danger, but now is the time to tell you why you were fighting and why all these people died." In not doing so, the authorities seemed to erase all the moral ground of this war. . . . By acting this way, the leaders overturned all the democratic rules, and from that moment you had the option of either listening to them or not. . . . They left no basis of a legitimate democratic country, and that was the time to act according to your conscience.

As the ambiguity of the war increased over time, the question of its justification, or justice, became the major concern of the soldiers. The refusers reported that, at least for them, the lack of a just meaning for the war had a strong relationship to their inability to overcome the natural fear of death. In the words of one refuser: "I am a paratrooper. It is a very scary job — I always fear the jump from the airplane. . . . but here, in the Lebanon war, I could not find the power to overcome my fear. I think I just did not want to."

Another subject said:

Before refusing I knew that the first question I would be asked is, "Are you scared?" and there was some fear; there is no sense in saying that I was not afraid . . . but I could not find any moral justification that would convince me to overcome the fear. I was afraid of dying in vain. This is a much bigger price than the price for social condemnation of going to prison.

Indeed, it might be argued that soldiers may die in vain even in a meaningful (just or inevitable) war. Yet there is greater likelihood that a soldier may not fear a meaningless death if a war is aimed at protecting fundamental values, national independence, communal freedom, and people's lives when all the other means to protect them are not sufficient (Walzer, 1977).

The above moral considerations seem to point out that more than in any other conflict, the objectives of the Lebanon war did not overlap with the justice criteria of those who had to fight it. For the subjects in this study, this justice discrepancy was crucial for their functioning in the routine discipline of a soldier:

Israel has enormous problems of survival, and we have more wars waiting for us. We cannot afford to choose wars. We cannot allow ourselves to wage wars in vain. A condition of going to war is that our lives are severely threatened. The second requirement is that we have done all we can to remove the threat. Only then I feel that the war is just and that I am obliged to do all I can to take part in it.

2.   The Moral Reality of the War

Whereas there is no way in which the individual soldier can have a direct impact on the objectives of the war, he can raise his moral voice in regard to the way the war is being handled (Walzer, 1977). Twenty-six subjects (72 percent) declared their refusal *after* serving in Lebanon. Yet the mere participation, combined with the fact that this was not their first war, gives no clue as to why only in this war had they found refusal to be the right, moral solution. As noted by Melzer, "To tell us again that war is hell is not to tell us why one should be justified in demanding for himself an immunity in advance" or the right to dissociate himself from it (Melzer, 1975, 54). The answer, then, seems to be more subtle.

The Lebanon war, primarily a war among civilians, sharpened the moral dilemmas faced by individual soldiers who were concerned about innocent victims. The study subjects were faced with situations in this war in which they could not simply function in line with the IDF traditional moral premise such as "purity of weapon" (careful and just use of military power; Gal 1986). They argued that in many cases even traditional self-sacrifice would not prevent the immoral action; therefore, they had to search for other moral solutions enabling them to preserve their principles as well as to prevent the possible future deterioration of the war.

The case of Colonel Eli Geva seems to mark the first step for another mode of moral sacrifice and further legitimization of conscientious objection during war. Geva, the youngest career commander in the IDF, was among those who were the strongest advocates of the war (though in its limited scope considered a retaliatory attack on the PLO bases up to forty kilometers from Israel's northern border). He became famous on the morning of July 27, 1982 when an IDF spokesman announced that Geva, who commanded a tank brigade (which was the spearhead of the fighting) up to the Beirut-Damascus Road, had asked to be released from his command and instead to participate in the war as a simple soldier. He objected to a planned military move toward conquering Lebanon's capital city of Beirut. Geva, who was considered a brilliant officer, claimed that as a commander he could neither accept responsibility for the civilian casualties likely to be caused nor face the prospect of justifying the action to the families of those in his unit who would be killed.

Geva's original request to the chief of staff was to serve as an ordinary soldier and not to leave his troops. His request caused deep confusion among the middle and senior ranking IDF officers, and it became a target of condemnation by many soldiers as well as the general public. The chief of staff accused him of abandoning his troops (*Jerusalem Post,* August 2, 1982) and the minister of defense claimed that many soldiers in his brigade had died because of his conduct (*Jerusalem Post,* September 17, 1982; also Gal 1985). Subsequently, Geva was dismissed from the army in the midst of the fighting. The planned operation to enter Beirut was abandoned as well.

Later on, when interviewed as a civilian, Geva explained, "It is vital [for the authorities] to understand the limitations of power" (*Jerusalem Post,* June 10, 1983). Yet he was not advocating refusal as a means for alerting the authorities of moral deterioration. He asserted, "One may oppose war but one may not refuse to serve in the army because it will undermine the basis of the army's existence" (*Jerusalem Post,* May 17, 1983).

Geva's arguments and action became more than just a dramatic public event: the rightness of his claims became more evident after the massacre in Sabra and Shatila during which Christian Phalangists murdered Palestinians in these two refugee camps — an action that came as a surprise to the Israeli public during the 1982 Jewish New Year holiday and indicated the severe moral deterioration of the war. Geva's mode of judgment and action struck many people on a personal level as an example of the straightforward talk and action traditionally ascribed to the culture of the young Israeli-born (Katriel 1986). Though there were a few cases of conscientious objection before his, none was known to the study subjects as being administered in public during an ongoing war, nor by such a high-ranking patriotic officer. For the simple soldier, this was a subtle legitimization for a new mode of moral coping. A refuser mused:

Before the Geva case, there was no model of refusal that a soldier could act according to. . . . Certainly this is a very radical action and in my opinion it has to be given in a suitable situation. I could never before think of refusal in my mind. Certainly not before the war . . . broke out.

No single instance of refusal, at least in this sample, is reported prior to Geva's case. It might be argued that Geva's inability to stop the moral deterioration of the war from within the military system inspired the simple soldier, whose options for changes are more limited (Gabriel and Savage 1981), to try and affect the system and/or simply to preserve his moral integrity from the outside. Said an interviewee:

> I am not naive. I do not think that across the borders there are people waiting for us with open arms. I believe that this is a terrible enemy. It is simply for this reason that I believe that we need to be even stronger and even more just. The moment we stop being just, we have no business there. I truly believe that with things like justice, you cannot play with soldiers.

3. The Occupied Territories

Metaphorically, Israeli selective conscientious objection may be viewed as rooted in the "seventh day of the Six Day War" — when the Israeli soldiers were left in the position of ruling over a population of a million Arabs (*Jerusalem Post,* May 24, 1982). Twenty-four subjects (68 percent) had the experience of serving in the territories throughout their reserve duty, and the service in Lebanon was a familiar scenario. One said:

> After serving in the occupied territories, where we had to enter houses and search for terrorists, I knew that I had two options: either to complain and try to change the behavior of the soldiers, or to take the personal option of not taking part. I reached an agreement with my commander whereby each time my unit went to serve in the territories, I stayed and cleaned out emergency vehicles. When the war broke out, it was mutually understood that the agreement was cancelled and that I ought to go to Lebanon. Then the question was not whether to go or not, but whether I should evade or refuse. I had a kidney complaint and both my commanders and I knew that I could get a complete release from the military service.

Since the war involved direct contact with Lebanese citizens over a long period, these experienced soldiers had no illusions that they could establish good relations with the native population. For example, a subject noted:

> Throughout my regular service I had a lot of contact with the population of the territories . . . but in those days I was young and I adopted the belief that this is a temporary situation as a result of a war and there is room for waiting for an opportunity to exchange territories for peace. As

the stagnation continued, my political stand became more clear. My thoughts on refusal existed already before the war.

As the first war since the peace treaty with Egypt, the Lebanon war was not seen in the eyes of the refusers as the last obvious option in the Arab-Israeli conflict. This officer explained his understanding of the situation:

I was too young for the army during the Six Day War, so I got the territories "ready made." Every year my brigade goes to Gaza for its reserve service. Until this, I had no involvement with the Palestinian problem. In my unit (artillery) there is an intellectual gap between the officers and the regular soldiers . . . most of them are Jews whose parents came as refugees from Arab countries and they really hate (the Arabs). They called me "Arab lover." Before the war in Lebanon, they would sit near the border with Egypt and play chess with the Egyptian soldiers. These soldiers in my unit did not even realize that their chess partners were the same as the people they hated.

But the complexity of this interaction is even more severe in practice, when the soldiers realize that they cannot pursue the military mission according to their moral code. A refuser related:

One of the major arguments against us is that if we care about the situation we should change it from within — that if you go to serve in the occupied territories or in Lebanon and treat the people well, that this is your contribution to the change. I cannot accept this argument because when young children begin throwing stones at you, you cannot just stand up and say "Just a minute, calm down." Instead you begin to run wild even though you don't want to . . . and then comes the unfortunate shooting.

Another refuser put it this way:

There is no doubt that though not on purpose, eventually what we are doing in the territories is violating the freedom of a lot of people. This concern of mine actually reflects the debate revolving around the argument that "we were forced to do so during the Six Days War, but are we *forced* to do it now?" During my compulsory service I was serving as an officer in the territories. Part of my present refusal is due to this service. For example, I was an assistant of a company commander and we were responsible of making curfew in Ramalla. . . . I guess we did not do vast brutal things but little ones . . . on a village near Ramalla there was a small road near a girls' school. They light tires . . . and there I am, an officer, heading my unit to chase them with clubs . . . we did not hit anybody, we just chased them inside the school and then I was thinking about all the transformation of the concept "Follow me" upon which we grew up as officers in the IDF. . . . The practice of this name is reflected in the high proportion of officers among Israel's war casualties. But those days, the *follow me* was bound to the idea of protecting the country. . . . I could never envision myself *taking part in such a scenario . . . with clubs.* . . . Even though none of my soldiers were hitting, I realized that is it impossible to create an "enlightened occupation".

The only option within this uncontrolled scenario is, in soldiers' slang, to "shoot and cry." To shoot, because it is the only way to save your own life; to cry, since you know deep in your heart that it probably could have been avoided. For subjects with experience in the territories, the service in Lebanon also revolved around this moral dilemma. In this context, refusal — *not* to shoot and *not* to cry — was seen as the only solution available. In other words, one subject said:

I always believed in making changes from within . . . I could never see myself as a refuser. But after all these years of "shooting and crying" you reach a stage in this inner war when all the conventional modes of protest make you a full participant in these actions because *you are doing them* even though you protest later. What would you say to yourself years from now "I was screaming against Lebanon but I went there"?

In summing up, it must be emphasized that (at the time of the interviews — 1983) the refusals of the sample were specific to Lebanon, not to the territories. As for the latter, most realized that this situation was far removed from their ability to make any immediate changes. However, this was not their feeling in regard to the Lebanon ordeal. Yet, after their refusal, some raised the possibility of acting similarly out of moral frustration in regard to the territories.[1]

4.   Moral Atmosphere of Protest

The war in Lebanon was the first in the country's history that exposed the individual soldier to a protest group, Yesh Gvul

("There Is a Limit"—see p. 36), which advocated and supported refusal. The declared action of this movement seems to have been inspired by the two extreme modes of political activism that developed within Israeli society after the 1967 war. Historically, the Six Day War, after which Israel found itself ruling Arab territories, appeared to be a turning point in the country's traditional operative consensus (Sprinzak 1977). A split emerged between the minimalists and the maximalists with regard to the fate of the territories.

This split, however, was not extremely visible until the 1973 Yom Kippur War. Soon after, both sides seemed to translate their ideological judgments into concrete actions by making some significant changes in Israeli society. The maximalists—together with the religious activists—headed toward changing Jewish demography in the territories by settling there. Their consistency and persistent, at times illegal, attempts to settle new areas bore fruits even before the right wing (Likud party) was in power. The minimalists, mainly ex-soldiers from the 1973 Yom Kippur War, succeeded in various persistent and democratic modes of protest to replace the leaders in the war government following judicial inquiry. After Saadat's visit to Jerusalem, mainly grouped in the Peace Now protest movement, these minimalists further urged taking the risk of exchanging territories for peace with Egypt. Both modes of action may have paved the way for counting on refusal: the individualistic lawbreaking taken from the maximalists' experience, on the one hand; and on the other, the recognition of the special weight given to a protest by the moral voice of ex-soldier reservists adhering to the minimalists' values.

Compared to the protest movements following the Yom Kippur war, which primarily concerned the misfunctioning of the government's handling of the war, the Lebanon protest groups surfaced during the war and focused their protest on its moral/ideological objectives and social implications. Overall, eight major movements have emerged:

The Committee Against the War in Lebanon. Originally founded prior to the war in order to protest against official policy in the territories. At the outbreak of the war, it changed its name and goals to protest the war in Lebanon. Its membership: Communists, extreme leftists, and some professors from Tel Aviv University, even including some who regard themselves as anti-Zionist.

Soldiers Against Silence. Founded a month after the war, when three officers and a pilot who participated in the bombing of Beirut met at a journalist's home in Tel Aviv and declared they were not prepared to die in such a war. A few weeks later their action seemed to serve as an incentive for a spontaneous demonstration drawing some 15,000 people.

Women Against Silence. Wives of soldiers in Lebanon who protested several times in Jerusalem as the war continued.

Mothers Against Silence. Formed three weeks after the war by mothers of fighting soldiers. Some 15,000 women signed a petition to "stop the madness" (New York Times Magazine October 30, 1983).

No to the Ribbon. Composed of a group of reserve soldiers who had fought in Lebanon and who urged those who also served there to reject the campaign ribbon issued by the government.

Protest Guards in Front of the Prime Minister's House. A group of individuals, some also members of other protest movements, stood in front of Begin's house holding a sign with the number of the casualties in the war, changing its numbers accordingly in order to keep the prime minister "informed."

Peace Now. The biggest and the best-organized group. It was not active, however, during the first three weeks of the war either because most of its members were in the army or because of its support for the strategy of the campaign (a limited retaliation against the terrorists). Its activities culminated in urging the government to establish a commission of inquiry following the massacre in the Sabra and Shatila camps, which brought almost half a million people into the streets and resulted in the dismissal of the defense minister. A large group of refusers were ex-members of Peace Now, who claimed that its conventional modes of protest were quite "anemic" and ineffective.

Yesh Gvul (There Is a Limit). Began as a protest against service in the territories shortly before the Lebanon war; it evolved on the first day of the war into an ad hoc movement pertaining to Lebanon, advocating refusal to serve there as the right, moral action. Its members were mainly reservists, some of whom called for future refusal to serve in the territories (*Ha'aretz* June 3, 1983). A letter signed by both reserve officers and men — and which was sent to the prime minister and the minister of defense — contained the policy of the movement:

We (15) officers and (71) soldiers in the reserve ask you not to send us to Lebanon as we can no longer handle it. We have killed and been killed too much in this war. We conquered, bombed and destroyed. Why? and for what? Today it is clear to us: through the use of war and military force you try to solve the Palestinian problem. But there is no solution to this type of problem. You are trying to force a new arrangement on Lebanon and to kill and be killed for the Phalangists (the Christian forces allied with the IDF-R.L.). You lied to us! You spoke of 40 km and you came 40 km from Damascus and entered Beirut. And still a bloody road awaits us: conquest, resistance, oppression. Instead of Peace for the Galilee you brought us war without end. For this war, these lies and this occupation there is no national consensus. Bring the soldiers home! We swear to defend the peace and the security of the country of Israel. We are committed to this oath. Therefore we entreat you to allow us to perform the reserve service on Israeli soil, not in the land of Lebanon. (*Ha'air* July 9, 1982)

In addition to the initiation of and participation in various modes of demonstration in regard to the withdrawal from Lebanon, the policy of Yesh Gvul was to publish each refuser's name and to provide financial support for each family when needed. Its uniqueness was reserved not only for the overt declaration of refusal as a mode of protest, but also for the fact that its membership did not consist of anti-Zionists or Communists only, but rather included fighting reservists.

Only 50 percent of the subjects were affiliated to Yesh Gvul. However, existence of a protest movement that advocated refusal seemed to ease the decision-making process of study subjects in various ways. For example, it provided a visible channel of action for the soldier with a Zionist and leftist orientation:

For a long time I have been a member of the left wing movement . . . and this idea has "cooked" in my mind for a long time. I have a long-standing dissatisfaction with what is going on in the occupied territories. . . . In this sense I am not unique even among those who did not refuse. You have to realize that refusal solved many problems for the left . . . For sixteen years (1967–1982) there has been a continuous feeling of dissatisfaction with the few ways of inducing an effective change and the channels of action have been gradually blocked . . . another demonstration, another march to a new settlement. Today, there might be quite a fuss over the refusers, but in the beginning at least, it was a source of joy for the Left that a visible action was being exercised while the Right held the power. Peace Now was virtually running around in circles searching for consensus, and here was a movement — There is a Limit — that could be defined as radical, and this movement gained much from the action of the refusers, many of whom were its members.

For a personal mode of action:

It felt good that I was giving my personal answer to the war in Lebanon. Before, I demonstrated, I signed petitions . . . but here, in the refusal, there was a possibility to prick the balloon myself.

A refuge for the undecided:

I see the Yesh Gvul movement as a bus which I stepped on since it stopped at the right stop when I needed it. But when it changes or I change directions, I will get off it.

A model of group action for those refusers who did not want to act alone:

In spite of the fact that the people in the kibbutz were against my step, the fact that there were fifty other refusers — before I refused — helped me. It is a big number for me: I knew that I was not alone.

An alternative protest group for those disillusioned with Peace Now:

For a long time I was an active member of Peace Now. I believed in making changes from within . . . But there is a stage in this inner war when a democratic game is no longer a suit that covers the body. There should not be any more talking, but rather action.

Interestingly, the strongest opposition to the refusers' protest movement came from the fighting soldiers (mainly affiliated with Peace Now), who expressed their worries in regard to the democratic values of the country in which the army is a necessity. Rightist activists, though advocating the war, nevertheless did not express bitter objection to the movements. Within Israeli society, this nonreaction attitude does not seem to be an accidental one. It was based on the assumption that if and when a policy of withdrawal from the territories was decided, the maximalists themselves would become refusers.

5. "Ansar": The Final Straw

The war against terror, however justified, is a war fought among civilians. It requires from the soldiers the almost impossible task of discriminating between civilians and terrorists. During the Lebanon war, this moral task found both concrete and symbolic expression at one site: Ansar. Intended to be a prison camp for terrorists captured by the IDF in Lebanon, Ansar seemed to include all the possible paradoxes of the war and proved the last straw for many soldiers, particularly the experienced ones. In the words of a refuser:

Ansar was the final catalyst. This was a different type of war. It was purely against civilians. I never knew such a war before. After two months of fighting, with a break of four days, I came back home and there was another draft waiting for me . . . and this time to Ansar. I wanted to refuse but I did not know how to cope with it . . . My commanders are actually my friends and I knew that they would substitute for me . . . so I decided to go. We came in . . . it was like a concentration camp for me: wire fences, signs and piles of mud . . . all the associations came into my mind. I told my commander that I was refusing . . . He asked me "What is the difference between manning a checkpoint and serving in Ansar?" It was hard to explain to him that this was the edge of my moral lines. I was proud of myself that I could refuse. I told nobody about it. I am not listed in the list of the refusers. I had contempt for myself before refusing.

Gradually, Ansar became a moral frame of reference for many soldiers:

Before my refusal, my commander tried to convince me to go, indicating that he would let me serve in Lebanon, not in Ansar. It became a kind of dichotomy, that Ansar is bad and Lebanon is good — but not for me. I said to myself that it would be better for me to sit inside the prison than to guard Ansar.

In an interview to the press, one refuser (who did not take part in this study) summed up this issue of Ansar: "The name Ansar has a kind of emotional meaning for me, a very frightening one. In this one word, there is all the badness of the war" (*Ha'air* April 22, 1983).

In the eyes of the refusers in this study, Ansar, which was also filled with terrorist children, was a practical and symbolic site, in which the futility of this type of war was exemplified:

The prisoners (who) knew that the Israeli soldiers as guards would not shoot at them . . . threw many things at them. Both sides were scared of each other. There were children there who threw bombs on Israeli vehicles. Nobody wanted to serve there. I was the youngest medic in my unit and I decided to enter the camp to do the job of . . . medical care. It was a hard job and I am glad I did it. I thought of volunteering again, but having come to realize that many things in this war in general and in this site in particular were not under my control, I decided to refuse.

CONCLUSION

This chapter has examined the socio-moral incentives for selective conscientious objection during the war in Lebanon. It seems that the just nature of the war, its moral reality, the atmosphere of protest and the specific experience of this study sample in the occupied territories — as well as in the civilian population in Lebanon — were socio-moral factors interwoven in the subjects' decision to challenge their assigned obligation to perform their reserve duty in Lebanon.

NOTE

1. In an interview with Eli Geva on August 14, 1987, in regard to the case of Elgazi, Geva argued that refusal to serve in the territories is a mistake. Though he indicated that it is obligatory for each soldier to judge any situation according to his conscience, he further warned that it is dangerous for moral arguments to be used in the wrong way. He said: "We are not an army that performs immoral actions in the territories. There might be some transgressions, but the army as a whole is functioning in a legitimate and moral way. The question of whether the IDF is a conquering army or a liberating army is a political question not a military question. Over all, the army is performing things that I am not sure it is happy to execute. But this is a political argument that the army need not be involved in" (*Yediot Acharonot,* p. 37).

Chapter 3

The Claim for Moral Superiority

Only 268 of the 3,421 years of recorded history have been without war (Durant et al. 1968). Yet, the attention given by psychologists to the decision-making process of combatants who refused to fight is relatively minimal. This is particularly surprising for researchers who adopt the cognitive developmental approach to morality (Kohlberg 1976, 1984), given its genuine concern with the individual's resistance to authority. The military setting, with discipline as a fundamental cornerstone, could have served as fertile ground for expanding our understanding of the way obedience and disobedience to authority are decided upon.

In spite of its being the only social institution in which individuals are not only permitted but expected to kill, war has not attracted cognitive developmental research even though, traditionally, such research questions the way individuals define their actions within conflicting, ambiguous situations revolving around the issues of life and law, conscience and punishment (Kohlberg 1976). When taking into account the growing interest in the relationship between moral judgment and moral action (Kohlberg 1980, 1984; Kohlberg and Candee 1984; Blasi, 1980, 1983; Candee, 1976; Locke 1983a, b), and particularly the contextual meaning of this relationship (Weinrich-Haste and Locke 1983), it seems that substantial attention to the way individuals reason and behave in relation to their military obligations might expand our knowledge about the cognition-conduct connection.

The complexity of judgment-action relationships has often been studied with trivial examples such as returning questionnaires (Krebs and Rosenwald 1977), cheating in tests (Krebs and Kohlberg 1973) or individual behavior in pretense distress situations (McNamee 1978). The nature of real life irreversible actions (Gilligan and Murphy 1979; Murphy and Gilligan 1980; Gilligan 1982) within social settings with significant ideological attributes (Haan 1975; Milgram 1974) has not been a major focus of inquiry. Exceptions are the analysis of Bernhardt's refusal to take part in the My Lai massacre and of Eichman's reasoning for his compliance to his superiors' orders (Kohlberg 1984).

In this chapter, Kohlberg's theoretical framework is utilized to analyze the refusers' claim for moral superiority. Whether refusal is the right moral response and resolution to the dilemmas faced by the Israeli reserve soldiers during the war in Lebanon is certainly a serious question that deserves attention. However, as suggested by Hare (1981), "People can disagree about the just solution to a particular dilemma, but there may be no complete just solution . . . " (p. 158). The real concerns, he continues, are the knowledge of the guiding principles of those who attempt to solve the moral dilemma they face. This line of inquiry is particularly attractive when applied to anyone who may make a claim for moral superiority, as in the case of selective conscientious objectors.

Given the nature of the actions examined in this book, that is, public, nonviolent, deliberate and rational law breaking, it is reasonable to expect that conscientious refusers would justify their actions on the basis of universal justice concerns (Cohen 1971; Walzer 1970; Zashin 1972), that is, principled moral thinking. Accordingly, from this ideal mode of moral disobedience, we can hypothesize that there would be a significant number of postconventional subjects among the group of disobedient soldiers.

Table 3.1 presents the Moral Judgment Interview scores and the Actual Moral Reasoning scores of the refusers in this study. A look at the table reveals that in the hypothetical context, the refusers' moral scores ranged from transitional stage 2/3 to stage 5 with transitional stage 3/4 as a modal stage. In the real life context, the refusers' scores ranged between transitional stage 2/3 and stage 5 with stage 4 as a modal stage.

Table 3.1
The Refusers' MJI and AMR Global Stage Distributions

MJI stage	2/3	3	3/4	4	4/5	5
	3(8.3)	1(2.8)	10(27.8)	6(16.7)	8(22.2)	8(22.2)
AMR Stage	3(8.3)	2(5.6)	6(16.7)	12(33.3)	3(8.3)	10(27.8)

Note: Numbers in parentheses indicate percentage.
Source: Linn 1987.

In the hypothetical context, 22 percent were fully postconventional with an additional 22 percent falling into the transitional 4/5 stage. In the real life context, 36 percent fell into stage 4/5 and 5. Although precise data on levels of postconventional moral reasoning among comparable groups of Israeli males are not readily available, the percentage of such people in the present study is higher than expected (Kohlberg 1984). Yet, statistical analysis of this data (Linn 1987a) fails to confirm the hypothesis that objection to serving in war was due to postconventional moral thinking.[1]

The major argument of the principled refusers revolved around the idea that though it is usually wrong to disobey in the Israel Defense Forces whose justice values they endorse, it is justified in the specific circumstances of the Lebanon war, which deviated from their existing beliefs regarding the objectives of a just war (*jus ad bellum*) and the way it should be handled (*jus in bello*) (Walzer 1977). Here is the reasoning of one officer:

I have taken upon myself quite willingly the obligation to participate in the IDF realizing that my country deserves freedom and that freedom should be protected. However, if the army that I serve obliges me to fight wars which are not defense wars but rather wars of choice, offensive wars, my entire moral commitment to this army is questionable. My second source of concern is related to the ways in which this army can execute such a war. There are universal criteria of human rights (including mine!) and the most critical touches upon the issue of fighting among civilians. I am not sure how these principles could be preserved in this type of war. Finally, I think that my moral commitment to the IDF includes my right to refuse.

When stage 4 was used as a cut-off point, a significant group of refusers were identified (69.4 percent). The construction of the action out of the minimum understanding of stage 4 moral logic may point toward an experience of soldiers' deep concern for the collective security (Emler 1983; Emler et al. 1983) and the ideal belief that the validity of one's moral claims emerged from membership in the unit (to which most of them asked to return after release from prison). This refuser explained:

I live in a society in which the army is a very important institution and I believe that every one is obliged to take part in it. Indeed a good army is an army which has discipline, but it is an army of better quality if the dedication of the soldiers is rooted in their moral concerns for those humane purposes that this important organization serves. At first I thought it would weaken the army if I refuse but I believe it has strengthened the whole system and as a member of the Israeli society I have contributed even more by bringing its attention to the limitation of "blind" fighting in this war — such a comment cannot harm the society and this is important. I guess my commander sensed that my worries were not centered on my principles only but also for the sake of the entire unit. . . Though he sentenced me, he allowed me to return to the unit after prison, as I requested.

Kohlberg's theory, with its "middle class American perspective" measure, does not provide a "culturally sensitive scoring" procedure as he himself has only recently acknowledged (Snarey et al. 1985). Thus justifications in support of "collective" moral resolutions can hardly break through stage 4 moral logic. Also, Kohlberg's scale is not sensitive to "nonmoral" factors such as the inclination to be *included* within the social system while criticizing it. His model praises the moral actor who can be "aware of values and rights prior to the social *attachment* and contracts" (Kohlberg 1976, 35). When this formula is examined within the Israeli context, where loyalty is critical to one's own survival, we might argue that the adherence to moral logic that reflects an impartial, outside-the-society moral view is, to a certain extent, a luxurious mode of moral perception. As one refuser said:

> I had the feeling that something was wrong in this war but I did not know how to change things, I tried to talk with friends around me to send letters, to demonstrate and then I realized that I would not solve MY problem until I refuse — but I could not do it to my friends — not because they would not like me after that (they really understood me), but because they trust me and needed me as well as I needed them — the biggest punishment for me would be to be removed to another unit — I can count on them to be around in times of war . . . and we would have such times.

The case of these Israeli refusers seems to delineate Kohlberg's neglect of an essential moral vector in real life action — the morality of loyalty (Linn 1986). Thus at the same time that the soldiers constructed the action of refusal (i.e., detachment from the unit), out of justice logic, 78 percent of them insisted on returning to their unit after prison. This tendency may perhaps explain why refusal did not emerge exclusively from postconventional, "prior to society," moral logic (Kohlberg 1976, 32).

Kohlberg's model further entails the premise that post-conventional moral thinkers are more prone to experience stage correspondence across hypothetical and actual social contexts (Kohlberg 1984). The findings of this study suggest that in the case of Israeli refusing soldiers, the correspondence in reasoning as measured by MJI and AMR scores was not exclusive to postconventional refusers but was manifested in the case of the conventional refusers as well.[2] Perhaps the choice of this specific action is more connected with the subjects' *isolation* tendencies (Linn 1985) or their courage to be alone (Fromm 1981), rather than with their stage of moral reasoning. Indeed, the decision to refuse was individually constructed; 83 percent of the subjects were the only refusers in their unit. It might be argued that the ability to act on the same level of one's moral competence is not necessarily the sole function of the more elaborate form of moral reasoning or the ability to reach an impartial moral view, but also the function of the ability to coordinate moral criticism of society as an *individual* who at the same time makes efforts to remain its member. Thus in line with Piaget's ideas that thoughts reveal themselves in action,

these findings seem to suggest that in the case of the Israeli refusers Kohlberg's justice structures reveal themselves in "individualistic" actions.

Moral reasoning seems not to be the only factor that affects
disobedience. This kind of nonviolent and overt breaking of the
law is also a deviant behavior that might entail some long-term
emotional consequences as well as legal punishment. Therefore,
the study needed to clarify how various attitudes, values, and
motives affected the intended meaning of the action and the experience of self in the choice of this action.[3]

The emotional ingredient involved in taking this deviant action
within a hostile milieu may entail different modes of self-involvement in the dilemma situation and the initiation of the action.
Whereas Kohlberg does not ignore behavioral and emotional components of experience, he considers that they are mediated
through moral channeling mechanisms. Thus an individual may
follow moral principles in a situation because he feels "they correctly define the situation, not because of an abstract affective
identification with these principles as verbal abstractions" (Kohlberg 1969, 231).

The extent to which the acting self is involved in the dilemma
and controls and initiates the resolution of the conflict has not
been thoroughly investigated by Kohlberg, mainly due to the limited scope of the studies. Most judgment-action research has been
conducted in situations of "resistance to temptation," where the
actor is required to break normative expectations for the sake of
self-interest. In this situation, the expected moral action is eventually that of "nonaction" when the ideal moral self is detached from
the other people in the situation and watches the status quo as an
outside objective observer. Bernhardt's reasoning for refusing to
shoot at My Lai may serve as a dramatic example of this "passive"
mode of involvement: "When I thought of shooting people I figured: Well, I am going to be doing my own war, let them do their
own war" (quoted in Kohlberg 1984, 549).

Less is known about situations where the individual is called to
break normative expectations on behalf of others, when the self
should initiate an altruistic action and when the moral resolution
needs to be found and constructed *in* the dilemma situation. This
mode of "active" self-involvement is represented by the case of

Hugh Thompson, an American soldier who accidently came to My Lai after the massacre and rescued nine Vietnamese by threatening Lieutenant William Calley not to interrupt him from pursuing a rescue mission (Hersh 1970).

Obviously, both types of self-involvement and action are needed in different (and some times in the same) real life conflicts. Moreover, they may be manifested on different occasions by the same person. Here, the action of disobedience, as performed by the Israeli soldiers, may be perceived by the actor as a response to a conflicting situation of "resistance to temptation" (not to join the crowd of fighters) or as a form of "altruistic action" (to prevent others from going by self-sacrifice). The rest of this chapter is focused on the examination of one dimension of the action's emotional components — that of passive or active involvement. In line with Kohlberg's theory, it was hypothesized that the higher the refusing soldiers were on the hierarchy of moral stages, the more likely it was that their emotional involvement would be active rather than passive.

The criteria for "active-passive" self involvement are presented in Table 3.2 (Linn 1987a).

An analysis of the data reveals that the refusers' subjective perception of themselves as having "active" or "passive" control over their performed actions was the only statistically significant independent attitudinal contributor to the stage of Actual Moral Reasoning (Linn 1987a). Moreover, when the sample was divided into conventionals and postconventionals (including transitional stage 4/5), it was found that whereas the conventional moral actors seemed to conceptualize themselves as passively involved in the action, the postconventionals seemed to experience active control over the action.[4] Examples of the active attitude follow.

1. It started with a feeling of restlessness . . . for years I used the conventional modes in expressing my disapproval of government policy but at the same time I continued paying taxes, going to the reserves and continuing to discuss the situation. By being a conscientious objector I moved toward another phase of involvement, that of personal involvement, a feeling that I am in control of my actions.

2. The apathy existed for me before the refusal. For me, refusal was a deviation from this state of mind. I felt that I could change the situa-

Table 3.2

Categories of Active-Passive Self-Involvement

Active
1. Emphasis on the self as the initiator of the action
2. Experience of competence in controlling the situation, the self is part of the dilemma situation
3. Identification of action strategy and consequences (did not surprise themselves by acting the way they did)
4. Emphasis on the action as a choice
5. Feeling in control of performing a deviant behavior

Passive
1. Emphasis on the self as detached from the action
2. Indirect control over the situation, the self is not part of the dilemma situation
3. No action strategy and planned consequences (surprised themselves in acting the way they did)
4. Emphasis on the 'no choice' nature of the action
5. Defending the self for being part of a deviant behavior

Source: Linn 1987.

tion and be responsible for my actions — I could even decide to go to prison.

3. I felt good that I could give my own personal response to the situation — to prick the balloon myself.

4. I tried to work in different ways, to convince my buddies to demonstrate, to write letters . . . they were all depressed. I knew I'd have to choose the most effective action since nothing was being done. I had to choose the most effective action and the one that I could act on.

5. I am proud to be a conscientious objector. I don't care what others think of me, It is much easier for me to defend this behavior than to explain to myself why I am going to Lebanon.

Examples of the passive attitude follow.

1. The one who took the stand was not me . . . I was passive throughout the whole action . . . Now, after performing the action of disobedi-

ence, we are all named by the public as conscientious objectors, as if we have taken the initiative . . . The truth of the matter is that the one who had taken the initiative was the other side — those who started the war and those who punished us and those who are fighting against us now — we just didn't want to fight against anybody.

2. I just could not wait for the trial to be over. I was waiting to be jailed.

3. I didn't believe that I had the strength to say no. I guess a person does not know his own strength until he acts.

4. I am just simply a soldier. I do not have many choices . . . to go or not to go. I can't even say to myself: "as an officer I have to go since my soldiers are going. [It] all comes down to my own personal stand — I have no choice.

5. I could never see myself as a conscientious objector in the Israel Defense Forces — but when I became one, I saw that I could be in this situation.

According to Kohlberg's theory, the attainment of postconventional moral thinking does not necessarily imply action. That is to say, the ability of a given individual to reason at a high stage level does not imply translation into action. In fact, it is almost the reverse: "the more sophisticated our moral understanding, the more difficult it may be to resolve conflicting moral claims" (Locke 1981, 177).

It is important to note that the subjects in this sample, are only those individuals who *succeeded* in translating their moral resolution of refusal into action. Many other potential refusers were either granted permission by sympathetic commanders not to serve in Lebanon or simply could not translate their decision to disobey into action (Linn in preparation). In the present formulation of Kohlberg's theory, little attention is given to the acting self vis à vis the principled self. The following refuser explains why this distinction is imperative:

If I had to follow my principles all the time I would find myself a prisoner of principles and in this situation you cannot *act*. I am not only motivated by moral principles but also by practical considerations: could I pursue the action? what is its effectiveness? how could I contribute to the whole goal of the country's security?

In spite of the interesting association between the subject's "active" attitude and postconventional actual moral reasoning, a comprehensive understanding of the action also requires contextual analyses (Brown and Herrnstein 1975). When judged within the Israeli context where the army serves many social functions far beyond its military missions (Gal 1986), an action such as disobedience seems to demand a more "passive" than "active" form of moral stand. The refusers were not the only soldiers who morally objected to the war, but rather the only soldiers who chose to manifest their objection by disobeying. Many more Israeli reserve soldiers who objected to the war on moral grounds chose to make an extra effort to preserve their principles in the battlefield and voiced their objection as civilians. They also knew that in Israeli society a special moral weight is given to criticism made by a reservist who stood up to his duties (Linn in preparation). Thus at least within the Israeli context, it might be argued that the action of disobedience is primarily the decision *not to act* (i.e., not to fulfill the obligation of reserve service and thus to refrain from participation in a more complex mode of protest). The refusers seem to be aware of this contextual mode of interpretation, as one of them suggests:

My decision to refuse was primarily the decision *not to be part of that which is being done*. There are probably many other ways in which you could prevent what you perceive as a wrong policy . . . In a way, I have chosen the easy path because it is easier *not to do wrong* than to do the right things . . . Nevertheless, I did it since I thought that the rarity of such an action within Israeli society would have an impact . . .

By analogy it might be argued that Kohlberg's context-free evaluation of Bernhardt's disobedience is not a comprehensive evaluation of the moral dilemma. After all, Bernhardt's nonaction ("Let them do their own war") did not prevent the My Lai disaster from happening.

Kohlberg does not relate to the content of the action, or to its contextual moral weight and to the different risks to the self. The refusers, however, indicated these differences when asked to reason on Kohlberg's hypothetical dilemmas:

In the case of Dr. Cohen (Kohlberg's first dilemma on form B of the MJI), the law does not instruct him what to *do* but rather what *not to do* (not to perform a mercy killing). And this is a big difference. In our case, the law instructs us to *do* something that is against our conscience . . . Here, the active part is the law that enforces the *doing* . . . and we say no.

Moreover, Kohlberg does not specify the extent to which his theory and model could explain the behavior of "doers" and "non-doers" and whether the psychological stress of saying yes is equal to that of saying no.

Though the findings suggest that refusers higher on the hierarchy of moral stage experienced more "active" control of their actions, it must be remembered that this "active" mode was measured, while "passive" action was the target of inquiry. It is questionable whether the refusers would hold the same level of moral reasoning and degree of stage consistency if they were called to act in more active missions such as rescuing a friend or an enemy woman from a minefield.

In summing up, it might be helpful to recall Gandhi's statement that "God never occurs to you in person but always in action" (Erikson 1970, 93). The findings of this study seem to suggest that the refusers' claim for moral superiority revealed itself by their exercising of an "individualistic," "active" action.

NOTES

1. The hypothesis that a majority of subjects would be postconventional was not supported. However, when stage 4 was used as a cutoff point, 69.4 percent of AMR subjects could support their action using stage 4 or higher moral reasoning; this was a statistically significant majority ($\chi^2 = 5.44$, $p < .025$).

2. The subjects' moral consistency, as measured by the correlation between MJI and AMR stage scores, was found to be highly significant ($r = .89$, $p < .001$). When MJI and AMR scores for each individual were compared, it was found that nineteen subjects had similar scores on the two interviews. Nine had AMR scores that were at least half a stage lower than their MJI scores, and eight had AMR scores at least half a stage higher than their MJI scores. The sign test allowing for ties was not statistically significant; this indicated consistent achievements on the MJI and AMR.

3. The two major categories of motives for refusing to serve are "political" and "moral" (Cohen 1971). They are discussed separately in Chapter 6.

4. In regard to emotional involvement, twenty-one subjects were classified as "passive" and fifteen as "active." Of the "active" subjects, nine (60 percent) had postconventional AMR scores, whereas of the "passive" subjects, only four (23.5 percent) were postconventionals. This proportion indicates a statistically significant association between being "active" and justifying one's own action with postconventional logic ($\chi^2 = 4.71$, $p = .02$).

Separate stepwise multiple linear regression analyses, with MJI scores as dependent variables, that included the demographic and attitudinal variables suggested that number of years of education was the only statistically significant predictor of MJI scores ($p < .00001$).

When AMR scores were examined as the dependent variables, both education and "active" versus "passive" involvement were statistically significantly associated with AMR scores. A change from "passive" to "active" involvement was found to contribute almost half a stage (forty-two points) to the AMR score, while each year of studies contributed fifteen points. Thus, these findings presented the action of disobedience as depending upon education and "active" involvement in the following way: AMR $= 165 + [15 \times n$ (years of study)$] + [42 \times 1$ (if "active") or 0 (if "passive")]. The following variables did not have statistically significant beta coefficients: age ($\beta = -.11$), military role ($\beta = -.11$), profession ($\beta = .20$), marital status ($\beta = .143$), "political" versus "moral" motivation ($\beta = -.19$), "protest" versus "personal" implications ($\beta = .05$), fighting experience ($\beta = .0008$), and timing of disobedience ($\beta = .18$).

Chapter 4

The Claim for Moral Consistency

The examination of consistency in moral reasoning is of particular interest in the case of conscientious refusal. This type of action depends upon some principles of morality independent of the actor and "to some degree (upon) his honest intentions and beliefs at the time of acting" (Cohen 1971, 211). In order to examine the actor's claim that he is genuinely and deeply governed by the demands of his conscience, we must primarily examine its nature and characteristics. Though there is no shared definition about the nature of the individual's conscience, consistency in moral concerns is often tied to the sincerity of the refuser. Childress (1982) describes it this way:

One major test of sincerity is consistency. Its application is, of course, easier in the case of the Universal Conscientious Objector, than in the case of the Selective Conscientious Objector, at least in part because the pacifist's commitments often entail a way of life (217–218).

The universal conscientious objector tends to refuse any cooperation with the military forces and in this way manifests consistency in various situations. The behavior of the selective conscientious objector, as has been illustrated by Scheissel (1968, 20), marks a "qualified acceptance of violence." Thus the measure of consistency is more intriguing when individuals who would voluntarily bear arms "refuse to commit themselves to any absolute principle . . .

(but) cling tenaciously to their right to judge (morally) each situation, each war" (p. 22).

One of the major justifications posed by a selective conscientious objector is that the specific action taken by him is the *only* one consistent with his moral code of values. There is some degree of consensus among social researchers that the most salient personal characteristic of conscientious objectors or selective conscientious objectors is indeed their ability to manifest "consistency" or "integrity" in their actions (Cohen 1970; Walzer 1971).

When deciding to detach himself from the shared moral meaning of the group, the objector often emphasizes that this action is the only way in which he can be "true" to his moral self; that "there is no other way" in which his conscience could remain intact (Tilling 1972). The validation of the moral consistency claim is not only the responsibility of the objector but also our duty:

> At some point, indeed, he may have to stand alone and defend his personal integrity against his fellow citizens. But this is hard to do and we ought not to pretend that it is (morally) easy. *Nor ought we make it easy* (Walzer 1970, 130, my emphasis).

In Kohlberg's terms, moral consistency refers to consistency in structure rather than in content: "People's verbal moral values about honesty have nothing to do with how they act. People who cheat express as much or more moral disapproval of cheating as those who do not cheat" (1970, 64).

Stage consistency is more likely to occur in the case of those individuals who are competent principled moral thinkers. Theoretically, the higher the stage of moral development, the higher the likelihood that the person would be able to act consistently with his or her principles since: "One cannot follow moral principles (stages 5 and 6) if one does not understand and believe in them" (Kohlberg 1976, 32).

As noted in Chapter 3, the Israeli refusers manifested an impressive consistency in the stage of moral reasoning between the hypothetical and the actual contexts. The refusers, most of whom had been in the past history dedicated and obedient soldiers (61 percent took part in former wars), reached the decision to disobey

(72 percent after serving in Lebanon) in correspondence with their moral competence.

Unlike the logic of Kohlberg's theory, which "suggests that as the structure of moral reasoning develops, it leads to a single, most just conclusion" (Candee, 1976, 1294), the refusers seem to reach a single mode of conclusion when holding various modes of moral thinking (though we should not ignore the impressive percentage of subjects who were functioning on stages 4, 4/5, and 5 in both contexts). Structural consistency was widespread among all the refusers.

Assuming no scoring difficulties, these findings of stage consistency point toward some anomaly where both conventional and postconventional modes of moral reasoning lead to an *unconventional* action of resisting, which was considered by the subjects as the *only* possible moral solution to the dilemma they faced.

How might we go about understanding the anomalous stage correspondence among the Israeli refusers? Following are several factors that may have contributed to this phenomenon.

THE SPECIFIC NATURE OF THE ACTION AS A POLITICAL CHOICE

Kohlberg's measures of moral judgment have been found to be highly correlated with distinct political orientations (Candee 1976). Political actions that were oriented toward the *rejection* of the adequacy of the system's conventional definitions were found to be more associated with postconventional thinking (Emler et al. 1983). In his more recent writing, Kohlberg (1984, 581) acknowledges that "It seems likely that the content of moral choice and the relationship between stage structure and content may vary from one culture to another." Within the Israeli context, moral disobedience during war is an unconventional action so long as the soldier has not been given an illegal command.[1] A flagrantly illegal command is an order that would deviate from the traditional moral foundation of the IDF of Purity of Arms (Gal 1986; Linn 1986), which demands careful discrimination between an innocent civilian and an enemy soldier as well as the just use of military power. This convention has traditionally been translated into actions of extra self-sacrifice in maintaining one's own moral principles on the battlefield.

Paradoxically, the soldiers in this sample (like the public that objected to their action) did not want to undermine these conventions (i.e., the postconventional principles of the IDF):

This was not my first war, but it was the first time that I began to question all the norms upon which I grew up as an officer in the IDF. I did not have the inner strength to refuse on the first day . . . not because of my conscience . . . I guess it was a matter of fear.

However, when the subjects felt that these conventions could not be preserved in this war (due to the nature of the war, and the unique difficulties of the fight against terror), they had no alternative but to take an unconventional action (i.e., to refuse).

This confidence in the moral functioning of the IDF was one of their major reasons for not refusing on the first day of the war.

I took part in the war but somehow I did not feel good about it . . . Nevertheless, I did not consider refusal as an option for action since all the time I said to myself: wars are not pleasant experiences and though I had to do things that I did not like, all the time I had confidence that at least the IDF is keeping the tradition of "Purity of Arms." This confidence was stronger than I am . . .

To a certain extent, by taking the stand of refusal, this soldier, like the others, substitutes the traditional IDF concept of postconventional morality. This traditional concept provides for saving or protecting lives by means of loyalty to a system of justice, in contrast to the concept of an individual who stands outside the system in order to maintain these values. In this way, some anomaly was created: both MJI conventional and postconventional subjects corresponded to AMR stages that resulted in one way in the construction of a single just and *unconventional* action of resisting.

PERSONAL CHARACTERISTICS
OF THE REFUSERS

Moral refusal of military service is known as "purely personal moral protest — though moral selfishness — which is sometimes the only resort of the principled but lonely man" (Walzer 1968, 14).

Indeed the refusers' lonely manner of action seems to characterize their ability to *act* upon their judgments and to maintain the same logical structure. 83 percent were the only soldiers to refuse in their units.

Kohlberg (1976, 1984) is aware of the fact that the individual's stage of moral development, although an important predictor for moral action, is not the sole variable involved. He delineates the crucial role played by the individual's "ego strength" (Krebs 1967) as an intervening "nonmoral" factor that mediates between moral judgment and action. Yet its function has never been elaborated upon or thoroughly examined.

Within this sample, the reference to the nature of the individual's inner strength as a mediating "nonmoral" factor needs to be defined as the courage to act alone or "personal strength" (Linn, 1988; see Chapter 5). The refusers' courage to act in a lonely manner has been inspired by the following sources.

1. Previous Experience of Successful Solitary Action

We were facing the Syrians and I said to myself: "I do not know what I am doing here, and I planned that if there was a sudden attack, I would crawl out of the side of my tank and not take part in the fighting . . . but then I knew that if it happened I would not have the determination to do so . . . the social pressure in war is sometimes irresistible . . . The decision to refuse was my second hard decision. The first was my divorce . . . They were two recent and close decisions, and they gave me the feeling that I had the inner strength to do what I feel is right . . . even if the rest of the world does not share my ideas.

2. Lack of Formal or Personal Attachment to the Military Unit

As a medic, I do not have a unit of my own. I am sent to different units. I was not surprised to find that there were many medics among the refusers. It is not by chance. At least for myself, I know that my original attitude toward military activity caused me to ask to serve as a medic from the beginning.

The ideas about refusal were with me and in my political environment before the war and I guess will remain with me in regard to the territories when we get out of Lebanon. I guess the refusal to serve in the territories which existed among few *before the war* reflects the *real* dilemma. *I was all alone* with my ideas during the reserves and I had to cope with it all alone since the people around me did not share it. It was finally, with the backing of other people outside my unit who felt the same, that I made up my mind to act upon my own conscience.

3. Personal Predisposition of Isolation in Dilemma Solving

The question of refusal is the question of the extent to which you are ready to do things with which you disagree . . . in order to implement the decision to disobey within the Israeli army, to justify it to people you may *want* to fight alongside in the (possible) next war, which may be a just one (for example, if we are attacked by a neighboring country) you need to have either a high degree of inner strength or to happen to be isolated from people.

The courage to act alone seems to be as clear a contributing factor in pursuing this type of action as is moral disobedience in correspondence with one's moral competence. At least this conclusion can be reached when compared to the lower mode of AMR moral reasoning manifested by striking Israeli male physicians who deserted their hospitals as a group in order to protest injustice (see Chapter 5).

OPPORTUNITY FOR STIMULATION OF MORAL REASONING

The refusers were interviewed after their stay in military prison, a place where each of them might be looking at his performed behavior asking himself: What must my attitude be if I am willing to behave in a certain fashion within a given context (Bem 1970)? Here is one example:

In the Lebanon war, there was a fear of dying in vain. After all, the price that I was going to pay was much higher than the societal price should I go to prison. This is what I am saying to you now that you are inter- viewing me. It is not necessarily what I thought then.

To a certain extent the refusers' Actual Moral Reasoning might be regarded as hypothetical moral reasoning, and as such, the findings of a "structural whole" (Kohlberg 1984) are not a surprise; moreover, during their stay in prison, these individuals invested much time in analyzing the correctness of the action and, eventually, might have developed a clear action strategy to be used in dilemmas that involve legal issues, rules, authorities, and formal obligations, as do Kohlberg's dilemmas (Eisenberg-Berg 1979). Thus it might be argued that their moral reasoning has been crystalized toward a specific *content* of action, as the following quote illustrates. In responding to the question from Kohlberg's form B "Should Dr. Rogers report Dr. Jefferson" (who "conscientiously" performed a mercy killing)? one refusing officer said:

You ask me if Dr. Rogers should report Dr. Jefferson. But I do not understand your question! I think that if Dr. Jefferson decides that the right action is to give the woman the drug, he should stand up and report it himself personally and not wait to be reported . . . He should explain his just motive for action though it is against the law . . . In the same way I see the refuser — if you decide that serving in Lebanon is not justified, do not find medical excuses but stand up for what *you* think is right.

THE NATURE OF THE SCORING SYSTEM

One important dimension of the action performed by the refusers was the fact that it involved a public defiance of the law. This type of dilemma falls within the scope and nature of Kohlberg's test and devised scoring system. To some extent it might be argued that the moral dilemma presented to the subjects in Kohlberg's test was abstracted from the refusers' experience.

An ad hoc examination of the way in which these groups of individuals tend to solve their real life moral dilemmas was made using Lyons' (1982) scoring system. The findings suggest that 66 percent of the sample consisted of individuals who held justice reasoning as the predominant mode of moral thinking, whereas the rest were divided between care considerations (10 percent) and both modes (24 percent). Whereas this percentage corresponds with some recent findings on the sex differences in reasoning, that is, that males are more likely to employ justice reasoning in their moral resolution of real life dilemmas (Gilligan and Attanucci

1988), a more interesting study would be the one that focuses on the interplay of justice and care orientations among those soldiers who objected to the war, yet decided not to refuse (Linn in preparation).

In summary, despite the fact that the refusers defined the dilemma of whether to refuse at different stages of moral reasoning, they acted in line with their moral competence leading to the actualization of the same choice of action. It seems that the self-isolating tendencies and opportunities for external detachment available to the subjects, their predominant mode of justice thinking, and the political/justice nature of the dilemma they were facing were all contributing factors to this consistency.

It might be further argued that the choice of a unified course of action (i.e., to refuse), matches the Kohlbergian expected dual mode of moral resolution even in a real life setting. Maybe the choice of refusal was less dominated by the subjects' structure of moral reasoning than by their tendency to adopt an "either/or" logic when faced with the war dilemma. They apparently perceived their options as either to obey or to disobey, to stay in the unit or to leave.

Overall, the concrete decision to disobey seems not to be a function of a particular stage but was undertaken in accordance with the individual's moral competence. Possibly, the decision to become a selective conscientious objector is more connected with the overall feelings that "there is a dilemma" regarding the issue of life and death that calls for an immediate as well as an individualistic response. Here is how one refuser sums up the consistency of his moral feelings:

You ask me what the limit of obedience to authority is? This limit is *far from the limit of killing*. This limit emerges *particularly when you approach those without a gun.* . . . That is to say, if you feel that the command you receive is the one involving *no dilemma,* I suggest you *disobey!*

NOTE

1. The Israeli soldier is instructed that it is his duty not to obey a flagrantly illegal command. This phrase was coined following the Kfar Kassem massacre. On October 29, 1956, on the eve of the Sinai campaign, a curfew was imposed along the Jordanian border. Many of the

Arab inhabitants of Kfar Kassem were returning from their fields unaware of the curfew. A unit from the Border Patrol fired on them without
prior warning killing forty-nine and wounding another thirteen, half of
them women and children. The publicizing of the event was delayed until
the end of the Sinai Campaign. The government denounced the action
and found sufficient evidence to try the battalion commander and eleven
of his soldiers. In October 1958, they were sentenced to several terms of
imprisonment. In his verdict, the judge recommended that the brigade
commander responsible for giving the orders be put to trial. This officer
was found guilty for giving an order in which the curfew was enforced
only with firepower. He was warned for this action and received a symbolic fine of 10 cents. The trial raised some serious controversies among the
Israeli public. Some were more forgiving of those soldiers who were
ordered to carry out security missions. Others were shocked at the willingness of the officers and soldiers to carry out the command literally,
without discrimination. Many pointed out that those who were really
responsible for issuing the command were neither persecuted nor did they
receive formal punishment. The phrase "flagrantly illegal command" was
coined by the judge at this trial and suggests that the IDF soldier is not
obliged to execute a command such as was given at Kfar Kassem involving indiscriminate killing of innocent civilians. Moreover, he is *obliged not
to execute* such a command.

Chapter 5

Conscience in War and In "Labor War": Refusing Soldiers vis à vis Striking Physicians

Extreme social events often reveal the most noble as well as the most base examples of human behavior. Such events also provide social-moral researchers with the opportunity to focus on the interplay between the structure of the individual's moral personality and the role of the social context in shaping real life moral decisions and actions.

Two instances of real life actions in two familiar social circumstances are examined in this chapter: the first is the refusal of soldiers to take part in specific military service during a war, and the other is the refusal of physicians to provide medical care to the public during a "labor war," that is, a strike. It appears at first glance that these are two distinctly different social events in which there are few grounds for comparison. However, careful observation may reveal some striking similarities between the roles assigned by society to these two groups, and the circumstances in which they are obliged to make moral decisions and actions.

First and most important is the existence of a direct impact on human life. Soldiers are the only individuals in our democratic society who, at least in times of war, are endowed with the right to kill. At the other extreme stand the physicians who are expected by the society to alleviate human suffering under almost any circumstances, and are generally prohibited by law to end human life, even out of mercy.

Second, soldiers and physicians are often expected by society to act on behalf of other peoples' lives beyond the normal call of duty. This commitment is ritualized by a deliberate oath taken by these individuals. Upon completion of their military training, soldiers are asked to take an oath in which they promise to fulfill the most critical duty as citizens — to fight for their own state (Walzer 1970). Upon their graduation from medical school, physicians are obliged to take the oath of Hippocrates in which they promise to "exercise" their "art solely for the cure of . . . patients and the prevention of disease."

Third, both groups often perform their duties as part of hierarchical institutions where discipline is often critical for effective functioning. In the case of the physicians, this is particularly true in hospital settings.

Fourth, both soldiers and physicians are often required to make choices between conflicting rights and duties within ambiguous situations, whether in the turmoil of war or based upon the "Knowledge of uncertainty and the art of probability" (Siegler 1982, 2178), that characterize the state of medical knowledge in many cases.

How do these individuals make their real life (moral) decisions and how do they translate their judgments into action?

THE MORALITY OF THE
STRIKING PHYSICIANS

Physicians' strikes are becoming increasingly frequent in the medical sphere of the industrialized world, but in terms of duration, intensity, and bitterness, "the Israeli experience is a landmark" (Greenberg 1983, 181; Linn 1987b). In March 1983, after eleven months of unsuccessful negotiations with the government, the Israeli Medical Association undertook a strike. Its goals were to convince the government to raise physicians' salaries, to reduce the extremely long hours of work, and raise the lowered quality of health care services that had resulted. In the first stage of the protest, the public was provided with only thirty percent of regular medical care. When after three months the government had not responded to their demands, the physicians submitted their resignations en bloc and deserted their hospitals (on the decision of the strike organizers) to "hide out" for three days. This event was called Code Belgium after a similar episode in Belgium where the strikers' demands were met by the government after the physicians deserted the hospitals and went abroad (Greenberg 1983). Following the imposition of mandatory emergency rules by the government, the physicians returned to their hospitals. Contrary to the government intent, no medical care was given. Instead, the physicians spontaneously started a hunger strike, that lasted for ten days until a settlement was reached. It is important to note that throughout the entire strike period, emergency treatment and surgery were available. The strike was originally widely supported by the public. By the end, when it left in its wake at least 700 undiagnosed cases of cancer, much of this support had been withdrawn (Greenberg 1983).

It must be emphasized that the majority of the Israeli physicians are government employees or employed by the Sick Fund of the Labor Federation (Kupat Cholim). Their salaries and working conditions, standards of care, and patient loads are determined by these agencies. The average Israeli is a heavy consumer of medical care and visits his or her doctor an average of fourteen times per year, the highest rate in the world (as against 4.7 times per year in the United States). The average salary is $500 a month for a basic 200 hours of work (Greenberg 1983).

This situation is even more extreme when examined in the unique context in which the Israeli physicians develop their careers. Like any other Israeli citizen, the average male physician starts his career at the age of twenty-one years, after three years of compulsory service in the army. Some male medical students, who are granted permission by the army to start medical school at the age of eighteen, are obliged to serve as physicians in the army for six years upon completion of their training. Six years of medical training are followed by another six years of residency. Every year (until the age of fifty-five) every physician must perform one month of reserve service in the army. When he reaches the stage of senior training, he is thirty-three to thirty-five years old, married with two or three children, and has already served one year as a reserve soldier. When he performs his annual reserve service, he receives only a minimal wage, which does not include payment for extra hours he may have earned if he had not been serving in the army. If he is lucky enough to compete with other Israeli doctors who completed their studies abroad, he may get a permanent job when he is in his forties.

The physicians' decision to strike must be viewed in the context of an atmosphere of drastic changes in Israeli society, mainly the increased deterioration in the country's economy (inflation over 200 percent) and the extended Israel-Lebanon conflict. Many of the subjects in the physicians' study (Linn 1986) served in this conflict, either on the battlefield or in the hospitals to which many of the wounded soldiers were transferred. The prolongation of the war resulted in further deterioration of the already inflated economy and was followed by demands for a raise in salary by various professional sectors in the work market.

Throughout the entire period of the strike, fifty male physicians from three main hospitals in the country were randomly interviewed: twenty-five physicians were interviewed before they struck the hospital and undertook the hunger strike and twenty-five during the hunger strike. Their ages ranged between twenty-eight and forty years (mean 33, mode 29.9). All had at least nineteen years of education. The physicians underwent the same procedure of interviewing and testing as the soldiers. The interview for each was done in the hospital, lasted one to two hours, and was tape recorded with permission. The first part of the interview consisted of Kohlberg's test of moral development (form B) and the second part consisted of questions regarding their right to strike, to disobey their oath, to break the mandatory rules, to report a colleague who abandoned the strike, and so on (see Linn 1987b).

Both the soldiers' and the physicians' protocols were scored blindly by the same qualified rater who had not done the initial interviewing and was not aware of the subjects' identity. The examination follows three lines of inquiry:

1. *Stage consistency*. The extent to which each group of individuals succeeded in justifying their action in correspondence with their hypothetical moral competence.

2. *Personal consistency*. The extent to which the action performed by each group corresponded with their judgment concerning the morality of the action.

3. *"Nonmoral" variables*. The intervening factors that bridge judgment and action.

STAGE CONSISTENCY

Since both the physicians and the soldiers have gone through the same psychological test of moral reasoning, it would be most interesting to start this analysis by presenting their scores on the Kohlberg test. Table 5.1 shows the distributions of the global stage score for both samples in the hypothetical and the actual context.

A look at Table 5.1 suggests that in the hypothetical context the physicians' stages of moral reasoning ranged from stage 3 to transitional stage 4/5 with a modal stage 4. Their stage of Actual Moral Reasoning ranged between transitional stage 2/3 and stage 4 with a modal stage 3. That is to say, in the hypothetical context, the physicians' moral concerns were more in keeping with stage 4. This stage reflects their ability to take the view of the system, letting their conscience be bound by their defined professional obligations. In justifying hypothetical behavioral choices, the physicians emphasized their commitment to an obligation, such as the one they assumed when they decided to become doctors. In contrast to this, in the real life context their dominant mode of reasoning revolved around stage 3. Here the moral reasoning centered on the desire to win social approval and to avoid disapproval. Further analysis of the findings indicated a significant difference

Table 5.1
MJI and AMR Stage Scores of Soldiers and Physicians in Hypothetical and Actual Context

Stage		2/3	3	3/4	4	4/5	5
physicians	MJI	0	2	16	30+	2	0
(N = 50)	AMR	1	27+	16	6	0	0
refusers	MJI	3	1	10+	6	8	8
(N = 36)	AMR	3	2	6	12+	3	10

Source: Linn 1988.

in the physicians' mode of reasoning between the two contexts (Linn 1988; 1987b).

The soldiers' stage of moral reasoning in the hypothetical context ranged between transitional stage 2/3 to stage 5 with a modal transitional stage 3/4. Their stages of moral reasoning in the real life context ranged between transitional stage 2/3 and stage 5 with a modal stage 4. As noted in Chapters 3 and 4, there was strong association in the stage of the soldiers' moral reasoning between the hypothetical and the actual context.[1]

A comparison of the two groups of individuals in the hypothetical context reveals that among the group of refusing soldiers, 44.4 percent were originally postconventional moral thinkers (when transitional stage 4/5 served as the cutoff point for this category). Only 4 percent of the physicians were postconventionals, whereas the majority were conventionals. In practice, the differences were even more dramatic. Whereas 36 percent of the soldiers were postconventional moral actors, none of the physicians was functioning on this level and some of them even regressed to preconventional levels. Indeed, if one views combat refusal but not striking as postconventional action, then the findings support Kohlberg's theory.

The soldiers' group is portrayed by Kohlberg's scale as a group of moral thinkers who managed to exemplify consistency in reasoning in their real life practice. As noted in Chapters 3 and 4, the findings point toward some anomaly where both MJI conventional and postconventional soldiers corresponded to AMR stages that result in one way of their practicing the refusal to serve, that is, an unconventional and precedent setting action within Israeli society.

The physicians' group is portrayed on Kohlberg's scale as a group of conventional moral thinkers, as their MJI reasoning revolves mainly around stage 4 and lacks such an impressive number of postconventional thinkers as the soldiers' group. This finding, however, requires some methodological clarifications.

First, the existence of few cases of principled thinkers among the physicians might be a product of a methodological bias due to the short time available for interviewing. Unlike the soldiers who were interviewed in their homes and were sometimes given up to five hours to elaborate on their thoughts and justifications, the physicians were interviewed in the hospitals between shifts or during the hunger strike and were only able to give one hour or, at the most, up to two hours for the entire interview. This procedure seems to reduce the chances of an accurate match between the interviewee's (unelaborated) moral reasoning and Kohlberg's criterion judgments in the manual.

Second, the stages of moral development were assessed from the subjects' responses to the first two dilemmas on Kohlberg's form B of the Standard Moral Judgment Interview (see Appendix 1). This test is known as an excellent research vehicle for eliciting moral reasoning (Gibbs 1978). However, this test presents real life issues for the physicians, as the dilemma tells the story of a terminally ill patient who asks her own doctor to help her die (should he let her die?), and the case of a doctor who conscientiously performed this action (should he be punished?). For the physicians, Kohlberg's form B dilemmas were real life ones, and as such most often a shift in the stage scores between the hypothetical and the actual contexts might be expected (Gillian 1982; Haan 1975). Alternatively, it can be suggested that the merging into MJI stage 4 "social order" might not necessarily reflect the physicians' hypothetical moral competence but rather a dual mode of moral concerns: on one hand the concern for human lives due to the physicians' awareness of the limits of medical knowledge, and on the other their desire for protection and support from the medical system, particularly in those many cases of helplessness in the endless struggle with death and suffering.

As for the physicians' AMR stages, Kohlberg's model seems to doom in advance any possibility of high scoring for the physicians since it is biased toward the "pro" answers — life is always recognized as more valuable than the law that protects it (Brown and Herrnstein 1975). Moreover, the higher the stage, the higher the individualistic mode of reasoning to be expected. Kohlberg's scale is not sensitive to the justifications of group actions (beyond stages 3-4). Thus even if the major concern of the physicians is to save more patients in the long run, their justification of a group action is less likely to be highly scored. An example is given in one physician's response to the question of whether the doctor should report a colleague who breaks the strike:

The doctor would not break ranks with his colleagues if he is a member of the medical association. He should do what all the other members do since this is a group action; otherwise we will not succeed.

Once again, the findings stand as a strong support to Kohlberg's theory in several ways:

1. One could not expect the physicians' action of refusal to be justified as postconventional action since it involved the suffering of innocent individuals.
2. It is not surprising to find that conventional moral thinkers are susceptible to personal and contextual influences upon their action (possibly this sensitivity to personal and situational factors may be a necessary quality for the medical profession, but obviously it might be regarded as a selective bias in this group of actors).
3. As forming and attempting to justify an *active* group action (unlike the possibility of *passive* individualistic action of the soldiers, see Chapters 4 and 8), the physicians' AMR reasoning might be regarded as reflecting their "realistic appraisal of the situation" (Locke 1983, 166).

Conceptually, the soldiers' dramatic stage consistency might be explained as the function of Kohlberg's exclusive attention to the individual's morality of justice. Within the Kohlbergian framework, the highly moral person is the one who "is aware of the values and rights *prior* to the social attachments and contracts" (Kohlberg 1976, 35). As correctly suggested by Brown and Herrnstein (1975, 325), this mode of reasoning "may be luxuries that only persons in privileged or carefully protected circumstances can afford." Obviously, by withdrawing themselves from their fighting units, the soldiers in this sample were able to maintain their ability to reason in this privileged "prior to society" standpoint.

As noted in Chapter 4, studies of political actions suggest that measures of moral reasoning are highly associated with distinct political orientation (Candee 1976). This seems to be the case particularly with those actions that are oriented toward a rejection of the adequacy of the system's conventional definition, which are more likely to be associated with postconventional thinking (Emler et al. 1983). Obviously, disobedience within the IDF falls within this category of action.

The physicians seem not to have the option for an individualistic, detached action of protest. Even if a physician declared his moral objection and concern in regard to the deteriorating medical system, it would lack the dramatic impact on the Israeli public as in the case of the soldiers. Even if the soldiers did not stop the war as they wished, they nevertheless succeeded on the personal level to preserve their principles and obviously their own physical lives. Unlike the physicians, their action did not have an immediate, direct, and visible effect on others' lives, a fact that may ease their ability to remain consistent to their hypothetical moral thinking.

JUDGMENT ACTION CONSISTENCY

To a certain extent, both the soldiers' and the physicians' AMR stage scores might also be regarded as "self-perception" scores (Bem 1970), because while in prison or while striking each of the subjects had the opportunity to look at his performed behavior and to ask himself: What must my attitude be if I am willing to behave in a certain fashion within a given context? (Bem 1970).

Indeed, the subjects' argumentation might be regarded as ad hoc action reasoning. Yet, it is important to note that both soldiers and physicians were in the process of the action performance while interviewed. The soldiers were facing another draft at the time of the interview and were struggling with the question of whether to "disobey" once again. The physicians were interviewed while striking in the hospitals, considerably before the strike was over (not knowing themselves how long it would last).

Apparently, both groups of individuals were performing an action of "disobedience" in choosing to say no to the command to serve in Lebanon and saying no to the government command to end the strike and to return to the hospitals. Yet, their perception of the rightness of their performed action was not the same.

The original decision to conduct a doctors' strike was made by the medical association. None of the physicians had *individually* reached the conclusion that this type of action, that is, a strike, was the right moral action. Unlike the soldiers, they had two sets of moral choices: (1) it is morally right to change the medical situation since people die of lack of treatment, and (2) it is morally wrong to strike because it is hurting the individual patient, but it is

morally right to join the strike because it is, apparently, the only
method to achieve change, at least for the future. Having found no
other moral resolution to the medical situation but to strike, the
physicians could not be wholly true to themselves while striking.

The soldiers viewed their action of refusal as the right and just
one. All claimed to act out of their moral convictions (though
differing in their definition of morality as a function of their stage).
They further claimed that no other action, except overt refusal,
would exemplify their objection to this specific war which was an
unjust war in their eyes. Most of them reported that only through
the performance of this specific action (and not the other modes of
objections such as group demonstrations) could they manage to
experience moral harmony or personal integrity.

I was among the first refusers. The time in prison was not pleasant at all.
The other prisoners did not understand how I voluntarily imprisoned
myself because of my actions. But somehow, it was only this action that
strengthened my ego—I not only felt that I could look at my face in the
mirror but also that history would record it favorably for me when one
day I would have kids.

The experience of self-consistency not only helped the soldiers
to face their own moral selves but also to defend their position
when facing the hostile public (which objected to the war, but
objected even more to this mode of protest).

The physicians, however, seemed to struggle with various sets of
moral inconsistencies, and eventually they viewed their action as a
matter of "psychological necessity" (Bem 1970) but they lacked the
experience of moral harmony.

The moral dilemmas are not exclusive for those of us who want to end the
strike. They are shared by those who preserve the strike as well. Every one
of them knows that more patients are dying in daily routine than in the
strike. We all feel so frustrated that we have to use the patients' suffering
for the future welfare of the patients and their doctors . . .

There were two levels of "psychological necessity": first, the need
to *act* (i.e., to deviate from the unjust status quo) and second the
need for *group* action. The physicians' original initiative was aimed
at making changes *within* the system as might be inferred from the

fact that the strike started after eleven months of negotiations with the government. Throughout this period and obviously during their absence from the hospitals, they escaped responsibility when acting as "part of the whole" (Frankl 1966, 72) to the point where they could distance themselves from their patients: "We have no other strength. We work with patients and it is not our responsibility if we utilize them as means." Without doubt this quote best illustrates the gap between the physicians' mode of Actual Moral Reasoning and those expected by the principled moral thinker who ideally perceives people as ends in themselves and believes that they should be treated as such. However, it is only if and when we view their behavior contextually that we may speculate that though they have performed the action, it was not the one they would ideally have wished to perform.

Viewed contextually, the physicians' neglect of the patients might be seen as neither their desired means for action nor the first tactical step, but as a conscious and unfortunate action in response to an *immoral* situation:

We are exploited by the professional oath that we take. Indeed, we are committed to save lives and to do all what we can to alleviate human suffering. However, this oath instructs us what to do in one sphere only — how to save others, but not how to save ourselves from exploitation . . . It is immoral to ask us to operate after 30 hours of non-stop work. All when we are underpaid and need to do extra work to make a living for the family. We did not initiate this immoral situation. It is time to tell the public the truth — more people are dying every day than in the strike.

The original motivating power of the physicians was their experience of self-inconsistency when they felt that their beliefs, principles, values, and accepted obligations did not correspond with their conscious performed action (Blasi and Oresick 1986). On the one hand, they wished to help the suffering patient with their knowledge, skills, and care. On the other hand, they were not able to do so because of the ineffectiveness of the medical system. Paradoxically, the very act of striking did not bring the physicians into the state of moral harmony they might have wished or expected. Instead, by channeling their action decision through a group mechanism, they simply substituted one set of inconsistencies for another, as they themselves acknowledged: "The tragedy is that our fight is not against the patients but FOR them. The fight is against the government which prevents us from treating them according to our knowledge."

This other set of self-inconsistency was not accidental. As noted by Blasi and Oresick (1986, 160), "to be self-inconsistent, the agent must intend to act contrary to his or her belief." Thus in spite of their expected self-inconsistency and moral "inconvenience," the physicians seemed to experience, by the very act of striking, some sense of accomplishment as distinct from the static, "nonaction" functioning. By forming a group, they seemed to regain the concrete ability to *act* (even if this action meant detachment from one's patients).

All that the public wants is our medical service. They forget to view us as human beings with families who want to earn at least as much as the teacher of their children in terms of hours of work and responsibility. I am not including in this claim the obvious service we should always provide, with no holidays, etc. I guess that by this strike, we succeeded in showing the public, but first of all ourselves, that we can ACT, that we have human needs too, and that we cannot go on living with a smile on our face while we are being constantly exploited and humiliated by the government.

Indeed, the acts of refusal, by both the physicians and the soldiers, involved the dimension of detachment. The physicians were able to detach themselves from their professional and humane commitment via the power of the group. The soldiers, however, were not military professionals. As reservists, they were actually dedicated "civilians in uniforms" who chose to become selective conscientious objectors (Linn 1986). By refusing, they were exercising their personal predisposition for an individualistic mode of action that involved detachment from an unjust scenario. Viewed contextually within the Israeli society, where every citizen is "a soldier on eleven months annual leave" (according to Yigael Yadin, a former Israeli chief of staff), detachment from the military unit also implies a detachment from the entire society and consequently an immediate threat to the actor's moral identity (Linn and Gilligan, 1989). Yet in spite of this threat, the soldiers reported that they reached a state of moral harmony in this specific, individualistic action that entails detachment: "I felt good with the fact that I was giving my personal answer to the war in Lebanon. Before, I demonstrated, I signed petitions . . . but here, by refusing, it was a chance to prick the balloon myself."

The rarity and illegality of this soldier's action seem to be a crucial part of the social impact carried with it within the Israeli society. Yet, in spite of the individualistic nature of the action, most soldiers admitted at one point or another in the interview that "I did not want to be the first." Paradoxically, their courage to perform an individualistic action seems to have been inspired by the existence of a protest movement that they themselves created, called "There is a limit" (see Chapter 2). Thus, though the soldiers acted *individually*, they nevertheless benefitted from the *group* as a frame of reference, even if only temporarily: "I see the protest movement named Yesh Gvul (There is a limit) as a bus which I stepped on since it stopped at the right stop when I needed it. But when it changes or I change direction, I will get off."

Moreover, although the soldiers decided to detach themselves from their unit, they nevertheless hoped to be able to return to the unit upon their release from prison, indicating that in the possible future (just) wars, they would want to fight alongside their long-term comrades.

For the physicians, the group action was not an option but rather a prerequisite for the public recognition of their moral frustrations. When they seemed to have no other option for action, the physicians started the hunger strike, which was defined by most of them as a mode of individualistic action:

We care for the patient as much as our government which issued the emergency rules. We respect our government and its concern, and we do not want to break the rules. By starving, we are doing the least aggressive act. Obviously, it is a temporary stand in this blocked situation. I feel very bad that I am on strike — in fact if I had to reach the stage of a hunger strike in order to show the public that I take a PERSONAL stand, it must show that I am not enjoying it.

NONMORAL FACTORS

Studies on adults as moral actors (see, e.g., Haan et al. 1968; Milgram 1974) suggest that the increase in moral stage does not necessitate stage consistency or judgment-action consistency. The failure of individuals to follow their moral principles was ascribed to the intervention of "nonmoral" factors such as "ego strength" (i.e., IQ, and attention) (Krebs 1967). Kohlberg suggests that "ego strength" or "will" is "an example of a factor closing the gap between moral judgment and moral action" (1984, 511). However, with the absence of detailed conceptual elaboration regarding the function of "ego strength," it remained within the moral psychological literature as no more than a "jargon of will power" (Locke 1983a, 23).

What, then, is the motivating power for the action of refusal both of the physicians and the soldiers in our study? In the case of an act that involves disobedience, it seems helpful to approach Fromm's (1981) idea regarding "the courage to be alone" as a mediating factor — the one we may define as "personal strength" (not to be equated with Kohlberg's concept of "ego strength").

The courage to act individually is one of the major characteristics of the soldiers across stages. Eighty-three percent of the soldiers were the only refusers in their units. This courage to be alone seems to be the major contributor to their stage consistency and/or the ability to practice the decision to disobey within this specific type of dilemma. A soldier explains it this way:

The question of refusal is the question of the extent to which you are ready to do things with which you are in disagreement . . . in order to implement the decision within the Israeli army, to justify it to people you may want to fight alongside in the (possible) next war, which may be a just one (for example, if we are attacked by a neighboring country), you need to have either a high degree of inner strength or to happen to be isolated from people.

Interestingly, within this sample of soldiers, the largest subgroup in terms of the military role were the medics (see Chapter 6). The medics were transferred from one unit to another according to the army's needs and therefore did not develop the same loyalties that others had to a single unit of their own. This contextual detachment might have provided them with the opportunity to invoke the courage to be alone in their action, a courage they needed to implement the decision to disobey. Other soldiers reported on previous experiences of successful solitary action as the ability to change a workplace, to get a divorce, and so on.

This was not the case with the physicians. As professionals who are preoccupied daily with the alleviating of human suffering, they could not envision an individualistic and deliberate abandonment of their assigned duty: "We are very strong when we talk ABOUT the patients, but when we face them alone, we just do the work. The government knows that this is our weak point and for years it has taken advantage of our conscience."

However, when realizing that change is essential and critical, they were willing to act in contradiction to their moral self (as measured against the patient's welfare). Trying to avoid this inconsistency, the physicians started their protest *within* the system, which is the only way in which they hoped they would be able to maintain their moral integrity.

It is further unclear whether the courage to be alone or "personal strength" is of the same nature when the moral actor is obliged to act within different types of social contexts. Is the same courage required by the protestor whose action calls for remaining with a group of other protesting individuals as in the case of the FSM (Free Speech Movement) sit-in arrestees (Haan et al. 1968)? Is it different for the protestor whose action calls for detaching oneself from a group of significant others, as in the case of the Israeli soldier?

The same questions might be asked in regard to the same individual—obviously for all the Israeli physicians who are also soldiers in the reserves, let alone for the one refusing soldier in the sample who was also a striking physician and considered both actions as morally right.

CONCLUSION

The two examples of disobedience within an extreme social context detailed in this chapter, that of refusing soldiers and striking physicians, are presented as an attempt to illuminate the complexity of real life moral action by the examination of stage consistency, judgment action consistency, and the underlying "nonmoral" motivating power. It seems that the soldiers' action of refusal is more likely to be performed with a higher mode of moral judgment than that of the physicians. Yet, the major characteristic of the soldiers' action is the consistency of reasoning between contexts across stages. At this level of analysis it is argued that this phenomenon might be attributed to the individualistic manner in which the action was performed. The ability of the physicians to perform as extreme an action as the neglect of patients seems to be associated with their desire for immediate change through a group action. The soldiers, who were afraid that their moral protest would be unheard *within* the system, had to raise their moral stand while being detached from their unit, an action that required not only an elaborate mode of moral competence but also the courage to be alone. When the two groups of actors are compared in terms of their "personal strength," it seems that the ability to act individually entails more chances for self-consistency, personal balance, and harmony as experienced by the soldiers. The physicians, who deliberately decided to act in line with the moral code of the group, ended up as actors who function with a constant feeling of self-inconsistency.

There are many questions yet to be raised and studied. What accounts for virtually 100 percent participation of the Israeli physicians in the strike (or alternatively, why only three physicians refused)? How could the fighting soldiers who objected to the war succeed in keeping their moral integrity? Is our democratic society more intimidated by those individuals who manifest moral integrity than by those who do not? Why is it that both groups of individuals (those who were morally consistent and those who were not) share the feeling that they still have a struggle ahead of them to convince society that they were morally right in their action?

NOTE

1. In this chapter the refusing soldiers are referred to as *soldiers* in order to distinguish them from the refusing physicians. When examining the physicians' pattern of stage shift between contexts (at least half a stage), it is learned that only one subject experienced upward shift, thirty-two experienced downward shift and seventeen experienced no score shifts. Comparison of the mean scores of MJI and AMR indicated a significant different ($t=8.52$, $p<0.0001$). Wilcoxon sign-rank test indicated a significant stage loss between the two dilemma situations ($p<0.0001$). Correlation coefficient between MJI and AMR was 0.079 ($p=0.33$), which is not statistically significant. The same analysis of data from each hospital yielded similar results. When examining the soldiers' stage scores between context it is learned that nineteen soldiers held no score shifts, nine

experienced upward shift, and eight experienced downward shift. It is learned from the AMR stage distribution that a significant number of soldiers (69.4 percent) succeeded in justifying their refusal utilizing at least stage four moral reasoning ($x^2 = 5.44$, $p < 0.001$). Correlation between the soldiers' MJI and AMR scores was statistically significant 0.89 ($p < 0.001$).

Morally or Politically Motivated Behavior? The Case of the Combatant Medics

In the military context, and particularly during time of war, the individual's "cry of conscience" is sometimes, though rarely, "publicized and concretized in the act of disobedience" (Cohen 1971, 12). When this action is performed in public through the nonviolent and deliberate breaking of the law, it may be defined as civil disobedience (Cohen 1971).

The moral significance of such action is to be judged by its external form and internal motivation. Cohen (1971) differentiates between two forms of civil disobedience, *direct* or *indirect,* according to the following criteria:

Direct civil disobedience, whether or not one believes it is sometimes justifiable, is at least readily and generally understood as being the protest it is intended to be. Indirect civil disobedience is very commonly misunderstood . . . They must somehow make clear to an apathetic or hostile public what the connection is between their disobedience and their social concern . . . Indirect civil disobedience will normally prove much harder to justify than direct disobedience (pp. 52–53).

Table 6.1 sums up the differences.

Cohen argues that a full understanding of any *actual* instance of civil disobedience requires an appreciation of the motivation of the disobedient.

Table 6.1
Forms of Disobedience

Direct	Indirect
1.The law deliberately broken is itself the object of protest	1. The law broken is other than (although more or less closely related to) the object of protest
2.Though the action might not be justifiable it is generally understood as being the protest it is intended to be.	2. The action is very commonly misunderstood. More effective when the connection between the act of disobedience and the social concern is most immediately visible.
3. Easy to justify the connection between the object of protest and the breaking of the law.	3. Much harder to justify than direct disobedience since depends upon the effectiveness of the action which is affected by the clarity of the relationship between the symbol and the object.

Source: Constructed from Cohen 1971.

For this we must go beyond the analysis of the objectively performed act, inquiring into the subjective and hence murky sphere of the character and aims of the actor. Civil disobedience is in every case the act of a conscientious person; but the particular principles to which that person believes himself bound by conscience will shed much light upon the entire enterprise, and upon him. (p. 57)

The identification of the internal motivation for civil disobedience is more complicated than its form since there are likely to be a number of principles involved for both form of actions, some of which the actor himself may be unaware. As noted by Cohen (1971, 58) determining the "real motivation in a particular case is, therefore, a messy and uncertain business."

The two major categories of motives for disobedience are political and moral (Cohen 1971). Ultimately, there is no clear distinction between them since political acts have moral consequences. Yet, as clearly explained by Cohen (1971, 58), although politics and morality cannot be separated, they can be distinguished:

Some acts and decisions take place within an essentially political framework, being addressed primarily to the whole community in view of its common concern. Other acts and decisions are more specifically personal, being undertaken by man for himself, out of chief regard for principles and values that he accepts as governing his conduct. These latter often have political import — import for the whole community — just as the former have moral import. But in being differently conceived and differently aimed, the two kinds of acts may reasonably be distinguished from one another, the first called political, the second moral.

Table 6.2 presents the main difference between political and moral motivation.

According to Cohen, moral disobedience is almost always direct, though it might be indirect when the object of the protest is a

Table 6.2
Motivation for Disobedience

Political
1. Wishing the action to be public
2. Referring to the action as essentially a tactic
3. Worried about the appeal of the action to the members of the community
4. Having as an external goal the changing of policy
5. Emphasis on the action's effectiveness
6. Focus on the act

Moral
1. The action may or may not be performed in public
2. Priority for ethical conviction. Tactical functions are secondary
3. Less ambitious than political action
4. More limited in object and more specific in intent than political action
5. Emphasis on the principles rather than the result
6. Focus on the actor

Source: Constructed from Cohen 1971.

policy not within the power of the protester to disobey directly. Politically motivated disobedience is usually indirect but may have its greatest effectiveness if it succeeds in disobeying the law that is the object of protest. Political motivation is not detected by Kohlberg's justice scale, which is geared toward the identification of the rational dimension of the individual's judgment.

At the preconventional level, the individual's moral perspective emerges from an egocentric point of view. Stage 1 represents an unreflective acceptance of rules and labels, whereas the command itself is never challenged. Stage 2 represents the judgment that recognizes a possible conflict between a rule and the individual needs.

At the conventional level, the individual's moral perspective encompasses the understanding of the origin and the function of rules as social utilities. Stage 3 judgment reflects awareness of mutual interpersonal expectations, relationships, and interpersonal conformity. In stage 4, the individual reaches the abstract, realizing the role of rules in the preservation of society at large, yet realizing that under specific circumstances disobeying the law fosters maintenance of the social system.

At the postconventional level (the principled perspective), the individual succeeds in obtaining and holding an objective and even impartial point of view on a morally controversial situation. Stage 5 embodies a social contract view of the relationship between individuals and society based on utilitarian considerations. Stage 6 (which does not exist in practice) is based on respect for the dignity of individuals as ends, and of morality as justice. This perspective entails the premise that when there is a conflict between the legal and the moral domains, the moral should almost always take precedence because it represents the more objective and impartial solution within and across societies.

Given the nature of Kohlberg's scale of moral reasoning, it might be expected that the higher the refusers were on the hierarchy of moral stages, the more likely it seemed that they would be morally, rather than politically, motivated (in line with Cohen's categories). Interestingly, this hypothesis was not confirmed (Linn 1987a). The findings suggest that with higher positions on the hierarchy, "political" motivations prevailed.[1] Thus it is questionable whether the minority of individuals, who according to Kohlberg succeed in obtaining the principled level, are indeed pure moral thinkers.[2]

Theoretically, the findings may call for further elaboration on behalf of Kohlberg regarding the moral sensitivity of his scale. Practically, they may serve as a partial explanation to the fact that, in terms of military role, combatant medics were the largest homogeneous group in the sample of the refusers (20 percent)?

How can a combatant medic refuse to aid a wounded person even in an unjust war? Is such refusal a morally or politically motivated behavior?

This chapter attempts to answer these questions by analyzing the motivation of each medic in the sample in line with Cohen's theory and categorization.

THE MEDICS

Avi

Avi was twenty-five years old at the time of the interview (1983) and a third-year student of philosophy who was fascinated by the idea of anarchy. He was a private and the only one in the sample who had been in prison prior to the Lebanon conflict, due to his refusal to perform reserve service in the occupied territories. After this experience, he was sent to a course for medics. When, two months after the official time of the war in Lebanon, his medical unit was recruited, he asked his battalion commander to release him from this service because of ideological reasons, but was not granted permission. His unit was sent to the most undesirable site for service, that is, to Ansar, a prisoner camp for the PLO terrorists, among them youths and children who were firing RPG missiles against Israeli armored vehicles, as well as civilians who were suspected of cooperation with the terrorists.

Though he was the youngest medic in his unit, he was the only one who was not afraid to enter the camp and treat the people. The month's service in Ansar made him think that if he were once again sent to Lebanon, he would ask to serve in Ansar. This service would fit his ideology; since the war is unjust, this is the only meaningful site where he could serve. However, when drafted he declined that option, indicating that sometimes the constraints of war are stronger than the will of the individual soldier who may find himself firing at innocent kids just because he has no other way of escaping himself. Avi feared that even at Ansar such a scenario might occur and therefore refusal was the best option: "Only by this action could I act on the mind of other people in order to enable them to see the futility of this fight against the PLO."

At some point in his inner struggle, Avi has reached the conclusion that the best tactic for refusal was cheating by presenting a low medical profile. However, he gave up this plan arguing that: "Within the Israeli context, you cannot act politically if you do not serve in the army . . . and also I am not a pacifist and would like to do my share when the objectives of the war are just."

Avi was sentenced and served twenty-six days in military prison; later he was dismissed from his unit. Upon his release from prison, he became an active member of the protest movement that advocated refusal (Yesh Gvul, see p. 36), and convinced others to disobey. Overall, he had a sense of satisfaction with his action: "I succeeded in 'being against,' and doing things against the will of others."

Beni

Beni was a twenty-three-year-old sergeant in a medical unit and the youngest subject in the sample. He was a member of a left-wing kibbutz which is located on one of the main highways to the border with Lebanon. He works as an educational leader for youth. Originally, as a gymnastics teacher in the compulsory service, he was not called to the war. However, because of the location of the kibbutz, he could not escape the scenery of the war:

When I saw all these vehicles going up, I realized that this was not a small campaign but rather a war. . . . I immediately called my unit and asked to be drafted, but I was not needed. A week later I was sent to be trained as a medic. Paradoxically, it was this six week course that intensified my objection to the unexpected continuation of the war.

His medical unit was not called to serve in Lebanon until ten months later. By that time he realized that the war had been extended from weeks to months and a year: "The war became part of our life. The indifference of the public worried me. Though I think the demonstrations were important I could not see how they would stop the war *practically.*"

Considering an action with an immediate impact on the public, Beni started a hunger strike in front of the Ministry of Defense, which lasted as long as he could endure it — nineteen days. The publicity surrounding his action also attracted pacifist organizations abroad, but Beni declined offers to become a member in their groups: "I have a realistic attitude — as long as there is a real threat to our country's survival and we are facing a reality of defense wars, I do not see myself refusing a priori to do reserve duty."

However, by the time he was drafted, he had confidence in his judgment that this was no longer a defensive war. Beni decided to refuse without any guilt feelings regarding his comrades: "As a medic in the IDF, I have no steady unit since I was transferred from one unit to the other according to the necessity of the situation."

Beni believes his disobedience was a personal solution to his dilemma of whether or not to serve in Lebanon. He regards the action of hunger strike as a protest. Unlike most of the selective conscientious objectors in this sample, Beni never served in Lebanon and this fact bothers him in terms of his ability to convince others that his action was correct: "I am considering the idea of serving *one* day in Lebanon in order to legitimize my claims when confronted by those who argue that I have never been there so how could I object?"

Beni was jailed for twenty-eight days and remained in the medical unit.

Cidi

Cidi was a thirty-year-old corporal in an engineering unit where he served as a medic. He was married and the father of a baby. He had seventeen years of formal education. He took part in the 1973 Yom Kippur War and served with his unit for two weeks in the first phase of the war in Lebanon, taking care of casualties. Cidi was politically active in the left-wing movement before the Lebanon war and had already considered the idea of refusing to serve in the Israeli occupied territories during his regular service. In spite of his civilian political background, he tried to understand the Lebanon war as a soldier:

> As the war started, I could not envisage myself as a conscientious objector
> . . . I was concerned about the strength of the IDF. Such an action, at
> that time, might have weakened this strength. I also knew that there was a
> severe punishment for an action of disobedience during war time. This is
> not the case in the reserves. I was all alone with my thoughts about the
> war and in the turmoil of the war I had no way of knowing how severe the
> situation was. . . . I thought that an effective protest should be carried
> out by many people. I needed this backing. Maybe I did not have the
> courage to disobey in the first phase of the war . . .

Cidi was called again in May 1983, nine months after his participation in the war (a month with twenty-seven refusers, see Chapter 2). By this time, the military and the political scenario was clear to Cidi: "I did not receive any explanation from my government why I should fight this war and particularly why we continued to stay in Lebanon."

Cidi told his commander that he wanted to serve within the Green Line rather than in Lebanon and that he, like any other soldier who expressed this wish, should be granted this permission. His commander, who was familiar with his political background, did not bother to sentence him. Cidi was sent to the brigadier who sentenced him to twenty-five days in prison and automatically a similar period upon his release if he refused again. Cidi was not surprised: "As a political activist in my civilian life, I already had the experience of opposing political policy. In that sphere, people do not like it either."

At the time of the interview Cidi felt that he was ready to serve a third prison term for his principles (which eventually he did). He also convinced others to refuse. His relations with his commanders are not good. In his words, "We have no communication at this point and therefore I would not be surprised if I was moved from the unit."

David

David was a forty-six-year-old veterinarian with nineteen years of study, who served as a health officer with the rank of lieutenant in an armored unit. He was married to a Jewish-American woman and they have three boys. He served in the Yom Kippur War but not in a combat unit. Like Cidi, David was drafted at the beginning of the war, although his unit did not take an active part in it. David did not consider disobedience during the first phase of the war, since he thought of the war as a just one as long as it was a short, *active prevention of terrorism.* He was also aware that as a soldier he could not be informed of all the details about a given war ahead of time. However, when he felt that the war stretched beyond certain limits, he became more skeptical about its purpose and nature, blaming the right-wing ruling party for using disproportionate force to solve the problem of terrorism. The use of disproportionate force seemed to create a value crisis in Israeli society.

I realized that my democratic country has to lie in order to make me fight. I guess it was the lies that made me a refuser . . . I felt like cannon fodder, and from this standpoint I thought if only I had the inner strength — I was obliged to refuse . . . what would I tell my kids years from now when asked "why did you serve in the war if you did not agree?"

And there was also the immediate fear of death and suffering as the outcome of a war that might not be a "just war": "I do not want to be in a wheelchair all my life . . . it somehow reminds me of those patients in wheelchairs whom I saw in Vienna during my veterinary studies; each of them had lost a leg while fighting on a different side of the battlefield . . . "

David did not want to actively refuse. He claims that he only wanted not to serve in Lebanon, like many others who were not looked upon as refusers when their commanders accepted their request to serve within the Green Line. However, when not granted this permission, he did refuse and was sentenced to twenty-eight days. At the time of the interview he was facing another draft to Lebanon, which he was not sure he would accept:

I have made my protest already, now I cannot be counted among those who say: I objected the war but I went . . . I would not choose to cheat about my medical condition nor to cheat in any other way in order to evade service in Lebanon . . . I acted this way so that I would be able to look in the mirror again and say: "Yes, that's me, I have translated my theoretical objection into practice."

Eli

Eli was a thirty-six-year-old sergeant, a medic in the infantry with sixteen years of studies, married, and a father of two daughters. He was a mechanical engineer, who at the time of the study was working for his master's degree in business administration. He is a long-term activist in the communist (anti-Zionist) party in Israel (Rakach). Unlike the other members in this sample of medics, Eli was the most radical refuser in terms of his political identification; he declares himself an anti-Zionist. He explains his military service as a direct outcome of the fact that he was born in Israel. He never served in the IDF out of Zionist identification and recalls that even in the compulsory service he refused to become an officer: "I could not see myself as commanding and educating soldiers and exemplifying to them the policy of a government to which I objected."

Drafted for the Yom Kippur War (1973), he and his unit were not sent to the battlefield. In Lebanon he served forty days prior to his decision to disobey. His unit's mission was to find terrorists who were hiding among the local population. Eli wanted to be the first refuser, but he did not have the courage to take this stand, or to suffer the severe punishment entailed in refusing during an official time of war. He refused when called once for reserve duty and when there were already some twenty instances of refusers. He was sentenced to twenty-six days in military prison and was later dismissed from his unit.

Feres

Feres was a twenty-nine-year-old physician, a lieutenant who serves in an armored unit, married, and has two daughters. Like Eli he refused to become an officer in the IDF. He demanded to become a medic, and explains how he won permission for this:

The IDF wanted me to be an officer, but I sought very strongly to be a medic because of my political stand. This was the period after the War of Attrition (1967–1970), and maybe the IDF at that point wanted medics with the potential of officers in order to improve the level of the medics.

The Yom Kippur War found him as a medic in an artillery unit on the Suez Canal where he was wounded:

I think this experience resulted in some changes regarding my perception of "no choice" wars. I realized that though we were attacked and the Yom Kippur War was a defensive war, it could have been prevented, if we had had the courage to deal politically with the Egyptians.

Since his release from compulsory service and up to the war in Lebanon, Feres was a member of the "Green Line" group, a political group that objected to service in the territories during their reserve duty. On the one occasion that his unit was assigned to serve in Hebron (in the occupied territories), he announced that his condition for service was that he would not deal with the Arab population but rather serve only in the headquarters, for which he was given permission. During the Lebanon war his unit was not drafted and he had time to direct the activity of the Yesh Gvul movement (see Chapter 2). When the Lebanon war broke out, his unit was not called, but Feres protested by refusing as a citizen to pay the war tax.

When Feres's unit was called to serve in Lebanon a year after the war started, the situation was clear to him, though he argues that he had a defined political objection to the war from the first day. His decision to refuse was instant: "I immediately called my commander and told him that I was not going. He did not wait. He ordered me to be sentenced to twenty-one days by higher authorities . . . I guess he did not even want to deal with me."

Feres was ready to serve a second term in prison, but he worried about his economic situation since, like all the refusers, he would not be paid his civilian salary by the army when jailed. Paradoxically, at the time of the interview he was fighting for his right to stay in the same unit, not out of attachment to his buddies ("both my battalion commanders would not talk to me anymore"), but rather for practical reasons: "They already know me. They would not send me to Lebanon! However, if I move, I will have to start all over again and convince my new commanders that my political ideas are just ones."

Feres advocates refusal as a political tool: "If five thousand people would sit in prison it would have an impact on the government. I am ready to 'sell' my medical knowledge to anybody who wants to cheat the army authorities for the sake of refusal."

Gidon

Gidon was a twenty-eight-year-old corporal, a medic in the infantry, and was single. He was born, lives, and works as a farmer in a kibbutz. He took part in the Litani operation (see Chapter 1). At that time, he was transferred from one company to another within his unit due to lack of motivation. He served one month in Lebanon from the beginning of the war and did not consider objection while serving in the first days: "Maybe, at the beginning, it did not seem like an all-out war but rather like a big retaliatory campaign, something like Litani B."

The catalyst for refusal was his experience as a tourist to a communal farm in Switzerland:

They were all against this war, like me, but when they asked me "couldn't you refuse?" I was shocked. I never thought about it as an option for me. At first I started to defend Israel, but then I could not understand what I was doing in Lebanon nor how to explain the Israeli policy.

The option of refusal has not left him since then. When drafted, he joined his unit late, trying to "miss" the bus to Lebanon. But the bus was still there when he came, so Gidon decided to refuse: "Why should a soldier be endowed with the right to kill but not with the right to refuse? If Begin wants to fight with Arafat, why should I do it?"

Gidon was sentenced to thirty-five days in prison and remained in the same unit. He was happy to be jailed and was ready to serve more time.

THE REFUSING MEDICS — MORAL OR POLITICAL DISOBEDIENTS?

The demographic characteristics of the medics and the nature of their decision are presented in Table 6.3.

Table 6.3 indicates that, for the most part, by refusing the command to serve in Lebanon the medics in this study performed a *direct* mode of disobedience. The breaking of this law was *directly* related to their object of resistance — the unjust objectives and handling of the war in Lebanon. Only one medic (Beni) was manifesting a different form of disobedience by initiating a hunger strike prior to his draft. Beni worried that the Israeli public was taking the war and its length for granted. Since he was not drafted at the time when he felt the war should be protested, he chose to make an *indirect* mode of protest by initiating a hunger strike in front of the Ministry of Defense. This medic, however, ended up performing a direct mode of disobedience by refusing to serve in Lebanon when his unit was finally called for this mission.

Indeed, the medics, as the largest identifiable group within the sample in terms of military role, pose some intriguing questions as to the *conscientious* nature of their action. Was it indeed a morally motivated or a politically motivated action?

A survey of the medics' decision-making process in light of Cohen's categorization suggests that they were mainly politically motivated. Some were already predisposed to disobedience prior to the war: Avi, Eli, and Feres showed some resistance to the military during their compulsory service. As for the others, although they did not agree with the objectives of the war, it was their perception of the moral deterioration of the war that finally shaped their decision to disobey.

The delineation of the internal motivation for disobedience was, indeed, much harder than the identification of its form. All the medics used moral arguments when attempting to explain their motives for the action of disobedience, though most of them were politically motivated. Their politically motivated behavior was not only a product of their civilian political backgrounds but also a by-product of their experience in the war.

During the first phase of the war, the medics, like the rest of the refusers, were reluctant to take the extreme stand of objection for various reasons: lack of knowledge (David), the fear of being the first one (Eli), the desire to help the situation (Avi), not being drafted (Beni, Cidi), and the belief that it would be a limited campaign (Gidon). Only Feres was a candidate for political disobedience from the first day of the war, as he also questioned his

Table 6.3
Medics' Demographics and Nature of Action

	A.	B.	C.	D.
Age, Yr.	25	23	30	46
Family status	single	single	married + 1	married + 3
Education, Yr.	15	12	17	19
Profession	student	educator	student	veterinarian
Unit	medical	medical	engineering	armored
Rank	private	sergeant	corporal	lieutenant
Service in Lebanon, days	30	0	14	0
Previous wars	no	no	Yom Kippur	Yom Kippur
Form	direct	indirect/direct	direct	direct
Motivation	political	political/moral	political	moral/political
Days in Prison	26	28	50	28
Return to unit	no	yes	undecided	yes

	E.	F.	G.
Age, Yr.	36	29	28
Family status	married + 2	married + 2	single
Education, Yr.	16	19	12
Profession	student	physician	farmer
Unit	infantry	armored	infantry
Rank	sergeant	lieutenant	corporal
Service in Lebanon, days	40	0	28
Previous wars	Yom Kippur	Yom Kippur	Litani A.
Form	direct	direct	direct
Motivation	political	political	moral
Days in Prison	26	21	35
Return to unit	yes	undecided	no

obligation to pay the war taxes. However, he probably would not have disobeyed in the first days, since disobedience during war time is an action that, within the IDF, is subject to more severe punishment than disobedience during normal reserve service. Feres at the time of the interview was already considering the option of cheating about his medical condition since he did not want to be imprisoned a second time when refusing another reserve service in Lebanon.

As the war became prolonged and as more military information flowed into their civilian life prior to their draft, it seems that the various restraints against disobedience gradually diminished. Yet the motivation for disobedience at this later point, usually ten to twelve months after the start of the war, was not identical in each case.

In most of the cases, it seems reasonable to conclude that the direct form of disobedience was associated with political motivation. Most obviously, those who were purely politically motivated (Avi, Beni, Cidi, Eli, Feres), were active in convincing others to disobey and were preoccupied about their effective public appearance. This was not the case with David, who was not eager to publicize his action, or Gidon, who viewed refusal as the most appropriate solution for himself. Though they seem to be more morally motivated than others, there appear to be some political components in their motivation. David is concerned with the fact that his action may be viewed also as *objection* to the war objectives, and in Gidon's case, his objection to the right-wing policy (as a member of a left-wing kibbutz) seems to have historical roots in his having resisted the fighting in the Litani campaign.

Did the motivational nature of the disobedient action make a difference to the army's attitude and punishment response?

From the case studies presented here, it seems that the disobedient actions of Beni, Cidi, David, and Gidon were more readily tolerated by the IDF than the actions performed by medics with a previous record of disobedience. These medics seem to have been tolerated and not transferred from their core unit (an option that in the IDF could be exercised by the commanders). However, it seems that the commanders were not eager to deal with political disobedients. They made no extra effort to try and convince such medics to change their decision (as was the case for those who were

observed by them as morally motivated refusers). Unlike the morally motivated refusers, the politically motivated refusers were not
regarded by the commanders as credible. Accordingly, there was a
difference in attitude.

Thus when Eli's commander sensed that his disobedience was
politically motivated, he would not talk to him. Cidi received even
worse treatment than Eli. It seems that his commander, who was
familiar with his record of political activism, did not even bother
to sentence him, but rather sent him to a higher authority, as a
result of which he had to serve two consecutive terms (and eventually a third term in the year following the study interviews). Avi
and Eli were dismissed from their units after completion of their
prison terms. The relationship of Cidi and Feres with their units
also was not stable.

This was not the case with Beni, David, and Gidon, whose
politically inspired disobedience was mixed with moral motivation
and overall seemed to be uniquely the product of the Lebanon war.
The commanders of the latter two seemed to tolerate their behavior.

For all the subjects, with the possible exception of Feres, remaining in the army seems to be a prerequisite for a valid political
or moral protest. Thus, for example, Avi would not lower his medical profile, (though morally he was ready to do it) since overall this
was not an effective tactic in the Israeli context. Beni considered
going to the Lebanese war zone for one day in order to gain better
validation for his political arguments.

Is the specific structure of the medics' relationship to their units
a contributing factor in the decision to refuse?

A careful analysis of the quality of the medics' attachment to
their units reveals, as explained by Beni, that they do not have a
unit of their own but rather were being transferred from one unit
to the other according to the army's changing needs. It seems that
refusal to serve in Lebanon, involving separation from the fighting
unit, is an action that is less painful socially for other soldiers
(Linn 1989b, Linn and Gilligan 1989). Alternatively, it might be
argued that the large percentage of the medics among the refusers
and their politically motivated behavior can be explained by a
selection bias: the tendency of the IDF to assign to the medical
(more humanitarian) units those individuals holding extreme po-

litical orientations. The lack of attachment to the unit in each of the cases presented here seems to contribute to their ability to disobey.

Like all the Israeli reservists, the medics are primarily civilians in uniforms; their actions need to be viewed as also reflecting their moral and political concerns as civilians. This fact might explain why they see themselves as responsible for the objectives of the war (*jus ad bellum*), whereas soldiers may be responsible only for their moral behavior in the battlefield (*jus in bello*) (Walzer 1977).

The negative attitude of the Israeli commanders to the politically motivated refusers, including the medics, seems not to be the function of personal dislike but rather the expression of their concern regarding the broad implication of refusal, particularly a politically motivated one. Within a democratic society, a political refuser may pose more danger than a moral refuser. The political refuser carries the message that the one who does not refuse is immoral and that this is the way all moral people should follow. In some sense, this is a dangerous threat to the entire system of the law. In the case of the moral refuser, as long as he argues that he cannot perform an immoral action, it is enough if we are convinced of the genuineness of his claims (Gabison 1986). But this seems not to be the case with the medics. None of them reported that they were ordered not to take care of wounded soldiers as well as the civilian population, which might be regarded as an illegal command that the soldier was obliged to refuse.

NOTES

1. Observers often regard the Lebanon war as the "Israeli Vietnam." This analogy erases the ground for explaining the unique phenomenon trend within the Israeli context in general, and when compared with the American context in particular. First, unlike the Israeli refusers, the American conscientious objectors during the Vietnam conflict were not necessarily experienced (reserve) soldiers but rather citizens who were called, one time in their lives, for service. By definition, these are two different groups of moral protestors. Starting from the Israeli example, here the protestors are individuals over the age of twenty-one, who have already completed three years of active duty. By the time they start their college

careers, they are already integrated into the society that they served. Their colleagues in the United States who are spending these years in colleges are, in fact, outside moral critics of the society. This distinction corresponds to Schuman's (1972) perception that the American students used moral rather than pragmatic arguments in their criticism of the goals and nature of the Vietnam War. As suggested by Schuman, this type of moral criticism is not surprising since these students "are intellectually more equipped to elaborate their sense of dissatisfaction with the war and to turn personal concern about participating in it into a critical examination of its goal." The general American public, however, expressed its objection, using more pragmatic arguments in showing their disillusionment over failure to win the war. This dichotomy of college-public or more precisely public-army, vis à vis college students does not exist in Israel, where war is a reality for students. These contextual differences also explain the recent surprise of American researchers when finding a large percentage of Vietnam veterans among the protestors to the war (Curry 1985), which is almost a given within Israeli society.

Second, Israeli citizens/soldiers who were facing the decision to refuse were facing unique personal and social constraints: their action of refusal had to be performed within a network of social relationships as the individual Israeli reserve soldier is entitled to stay in his unit for many years. Also, unlike the United States, Israel holds a mutual border with its enemy, a fact that makes the decision to refuse somehow a stronger moral dilemma.

Finally, there is a different moral atmosphere within the two countries in regard to the military service (obviously out of the military necessity). In the eyes of the Israeli public, service in the army is viewed positively and the army is viewed as a crucial social institution far beyond its military roles. This is not the same in the United States.

2. Of the 36 subjects, 12 were identified as having a "political" motivation (4 of these were postconventional); 15 had a "moral" motivation (3 of these were postconventional); 6 had both motivations (all were postconventional); and 3 could not be classified (all were preconventional). The chi-square test, after those with both attitudes or unclassified attitudes (total of 27 subjects) were excluded, was not significant ($\chi^2 = 0.12$, $p = .731$).

The Claim for Credibility

It appears that motivation is the single crucial factor that tears the average Israeli male citizen away from his civilian life and pushes him into the army life for one month per year for an average of two dozen years. Though this service is required by law, the realization of the necessity of defending the country (almost unquestionable until the war in Lebanon), as well as the life-long connection with members of the unit, seem to be strong contributing factors to the high percentage of service in the reserve service (Gal 1986).

When examined in terms of the individual's prospective life span, the average male citizen completes an average of at least an additional two years of army service on top of his three years of compulsory service. This calculation portrays only the minimal period of military service in the reserves. It does not include the unexpected and sudden long-term reserve service of up to six months during the Yom Kippur War, or the two to three months during the war in Lebanon.

Since the Israeli reservist is primarily a citizen in uniform, he knows he must expect that this duty may stand in conflict with some events in the routine of his civilian life. Thus, for example, it is not always easy to miss final exams as a university student, to leave the apples unpicked on the trees as a farmer, to leave behind a pregnant wife, a sick child, or an old, dependent mother without any economic incentives and with compensation given for basic salary only.

What the extreme orthodox in Israel can do legally in terms of evading military service (Blatt, et al. 1975), the secular, unmotivated male citizen cannot. Yet he can evade service by utilizing various excuses such as a special request from his work place, traveling abroad, or, more dramatically, changes in his medical profile.[1] Nevertheless, in spite of the accumulation of the military burden, the reservist's commitment to the army remains relatively high. There is room to believe that in terms of life-span service, the moral perspective undergoes some transformation as well, more likely toward the realization of the complexity of the moral dilemmas each war entails.[2]

In case of personal difficulties, the potential reservist may submit an appeal for release to a special committee (Valtam, meaning in Hebrew "the Committee for Coordination of Release from the reserve service), which might release him from the assigned service if the appeal is found justified. Yet, the reservist who is attached to his unit would take into consideration the conditions for delaying his service: he would have to fulfill his duty with another unit at another time. Given the fact that the life-long connection with the members of the unit might become, for some, the most appealing issue in the service, many would be reluctant to evade this transfer whenever or wherever possible.

The desire of the individual secular soldier not to participate in a given reserve service because it would contradict the dictate of his conscience is not recognized or accepted by the law nor by Valtam. The only way the individual soldier may present a request for release on moral grounds is during the special commander day before the battalion leaves for service, when the battalion commander usually devotes a special time to discuss ad hoc problems of release among the soldiers in the unit.

Who should have priority in obtaining a release? the one who has a sick child, a dependent mother, job difficulties, a pregnant wife, or one whose physical and personal life are all right but who is reluctant to serve with the unit because of severe moral concerns?

Obviously, the commander's task of devising a "just release scale" is not a simple one, nor is the task of devising an alternative scale for assessing the one soldier or the many soldiers who ask to be released on moral grounds. The art of assessing an individual's moral pain is not an easy one, as noted by Melzer (1975): "The task of clarifying the concept of 'acting conscientiously' is itself very difficult, let alone the task of judging conscientiousness in particular cases — questions to which God alone can know the answer" (p. 174).

Though they may differ in nature, both scales are but the first stage of assessment for release. The second is a joint moral concern: the question of credibility (Feeney 1987). Is the individual soldier's testimony entitled to be believed? And if so, to what extent? This chapter is an attempt to focus on the construction of a justice/credibility scale as has been done by the Israeli commanders of the refusers.

CREDIBILITY AND MORALITY

The prima facie obligation to obey the law in a lawful, democratic country is particularly binding upon the individual citizen. However, actual obligation in a specific complex situation may require the careful weighing of "many prima facie obligations, some of which may conflict head on with others" (Cohen 1971, 6). On becoming a disobedient, and particularly in the case of the selective conscientious objector, where refusal to do military service is not the rule but rather the extreme response to an injustice of a specific situation, the identification of the moral argument in support of this deviant action is a fundamental prerequisite. Moreover, since the action is primarily viewed as that of disobedience, the conduct is prima facie wrong and the burden of proving its moral correctness rests upon the actor. Assuming that such an action is performed reflectively and deliberately, there is room to believe that the disobedient is prepared to carry this burden.

As a moral actor, the refuser knows (and often wishes) that his action is not performed in a social vacuum. He knows that at some point he will have an audience to which he will have to explain the motives of his action and for whom he will also want to help interpret his actions (Goffman 1959). At the same time the audience will have the right and obligation to know why he chose to act above the dictate of the law. How credible are these claims? Cohen (1971) argues: "A man's belief about the moral character of his own act is surely not the only court before which that act may be

judged. But a reflective conscience is one court, and a very important one. Doing what one honestly thinks one is obligated to do is
not a sufficient condition of a morally honorable act, but it is a
necessary condition of such moral honor" (p. 21).

With the exception of a few situations, disobedience was not the
immediate solution to the moral struggle of the soldiers in this
sample. Primarily, they did not want to serve in Lebanon, hoping
that their request would be granted by their commanders. The
only way the commanders could use legal power in response to this
stand was to order the soldier to go to Lebanon, and when he
refused, to sentence him to up to thirty-five days in military prison
for committing a disciplinary offense.

In spite of the time pressure (often the final decision to refuse
was on the very day of leaving for service), it is learned from the
refusers that most of the commanders did not make automatic use
of their legal power or of the maximum punishment it entails.
From the refusers' reports it is learned that several reasons might
be responsible for this widespread attitude. First, in many cases
the commanders themselves realized that the soldier was not mere-
ly performing a disciplinary offense, thus the immediate utiliza-
tion of legal power was not the most adequate response. Second,
instead of immediate sentencing, the commanders chose to invest
much time in trying to persuade the soldier to withdraw from his
stubborn position. By this, they conveyed an implicit attitude of
some respect for his action. Third, the commanders realized that
they would not be able to perform their task with a rebellious
soldier. Thus, an attempt was made by them to learn about the
feelings of the soldier and to try to show him how he could function
in line with his moral concerns. Yet, they would finally sentence
him so as to prevent others from erroneously believing that this
might also be a way of release for themselves. Fourth, it might be
speculated that by not hurrying to sentence the soldiers, and by
not exercising their full power, the commanders conveyed to their
superiors their hidden objection to the war and/or their criticism
regarding an assigned mission with which they were not totally at
peace.

Left alone with the task of clarifying the concept of "acting
conscientiously," the commanders, quite intuitively, followed two
lines of inquiry: attempting to identify whether the act of the

soldier was indeed an action of disobedience caused by or associated with moral pain, and judging the rightness of the action. The commanders realized that these soldiers needed time in order to verbalize those nonlegal considerations that overrode their obligation to obey. Cohen explains: "The disobedient protester, to justify his action, must give extralegal reasons for breaking the law, and he must show that these nonlegal considerations override his obligation to obey the law. This will not be easy for him to do" (Cohen 1971, 102).

Crucial to this explanation is the realization that such lawbreaking requires the ability to present a rational defense (most preferable principled mode of thinking in Kohlberg's terms), or at least the understanding of the illegality of the action (stage 4 moral logic). The subjects of this study seem to follow these criteria, as a significant number (69.4 percent) of them were able to follow Kohlberg's stage 4, 4/5, and 5 moral logic. One refusing officer clarifies this point:

I do not believe that I am holding an a priori right to refuse—I guess what ought to be explained is the obligation to serve. The moment there is no clear obligation to serve, one may start thinking about the right to refuse, and one has to think thoroughly whether he is going to actualize this right. The exercising of this right involves a violation of the law and then, regretfully, I have to decide whether what I am called on to do is so terrible that it gives me the right to break the law.

I believe that the scale starts from the point where the IDF soldiers were ordered to help picking apples from the trees in the Kibbutz—here the IDF is being utilized to serve a purpose which is not pure self-defense. To send the IDF to serve in Lebanon is the same type of misuse of the army which I have the right and obligation to protest. . . . At the same time I am aware of the fact that when using my conscience as the guide to my action, I am not free, a priori from punishment. I believe that the very specific circumstances of the Lebanon war do not justify punishment for people like myself—yet I am ready for punishment and realize that if I am found wrong—I should be punished.

Another refusing soldier put it this way:

The interesting thing about the IDF refusers is that it is the law that caused them to deviate from the status quo . . . in the name of the law we were asked to take part in an unjust war. . . . The government, in the name of the law, sends so many soldiers to risk their lives, and the lives of others for a purely political purpose. Everybody reminds us that so far 560 to 580 IDF soldiers have been killed. Nobody mentions that about 20,000 have been killed from the other side — and we ought to know the moral justification for our toll of deaths on both sides. But even if no one from our side died and only *one* died from the other side we have the right to know why. . . . I believe that in a democratic regime, there is only one situation in which I should be asked to do such a drastic thing as to kill others in the name of my country: when there is an immediate and realistic threat to the existence of the nation.

The mere fact that an action was performed out of conscience obviously deserves our consideration. However, conscientious action is not necessarily a good action, nor is it an a priori genuine one.

However difficult to determine, that rightness will depend upon some principles of morality independent of the actor *and,* to some degree, his honest intentions and beliefs at the time of acting. But a third, and equally important matter upon which judgement must also sometimes be given is the moral character of the actor. Wrong acts are often done by good men. And that a man is governed, genuinely and deeply by the demands of his conscience is one factor (but not the only one) that we properly weigh in judging his goodness. (Cohen 1971, 212)

Lacking historical perspective, the refuser should be prepared for a feeling of uncertainty regarding the rightness of the action: "How can he be certain that he is right? What if the principles for which he spends his courage and stakes his life turn out to be silly, trivial or fanatic?" (Walzer 1970, 130).

This uncertainty must be shared also by those who sentence him given the fact that the rightness of such moral action is known to "remain perennially a subject of philosophical and political dispute" (Cohen 1971, 102). For the action to be morally right, it should entail two basic qualities in line with Kohlberg's philosophy: "(a) that is 'objectively right' in the sense that the use of philosophic principles by stage 5 reasoners leads to agreement on what constitutes 'right' action and (b) that is 'subjectively right' if it is both guided by a moral judgement or reason that is 'right' in form and consistent with the objectively right choice" (Kohlberg 1984, 259–260).

The identification of both qualities is not free from bias. Kohlberg's test, measuring the way in which the individual prescribes and values the socially good and right, that is, the individual's moral judgment, is assumed to be able to penetrate beyond the subject's opinions, attitudes, or beliefs to the reasoning or justifications that seem to direct his decision. Kohlberg's test, however, seems to favor the most verbal and better educated subjects. Yet, when assuming the selective conscientious objector to be most articulate about his action, holding "reflective considerations of means and ends" (Cohen 1968, 279), this bias might be negligible.

More specifically, the selective conscientious objector should be able to explain how and in what way his action is *not* contempt for the law nor is it a selfish interest, or an action that suggests that he take the law into his own hands, an action that undermines respect for the law, a self-defeating action, an action that cannot be justified when lawful channels remain open, or an action that subverts the democratic process (Cohen 1971).

While contemplating these necessary explanations, we should simultaneously examine their credibility following Childress' suggestion: "The principle of respect for persons does not require respect for the insincere conscience" (Childress 1982, 215).

THE SEARCH FOR CREDIBILITY

The decision to become a selective conscientious objector is primarily the decision *not* to do a certain act at a certain time. Hannah Arendt defines this Socratic logic as follows.

These are the rules of conscience, and they are—like those Thoreau announced in his essay—entirely negative. They do not say what to do; they say what not to do. They do not spell out certain principles for taking action; they lay down the boundaries no act should transgress. They say: Don't do wrong, for then you will have to live together with a wrongdoer. (Arendt 1972, 63)

In operative terms, an action that follows this logic need not be accepted a priori, as Cohen explains: "If in obeying his conscience another man is obliged to do what he believes—in good conscience — to be morally wrong, the genuineness of that conflict must give us a pause" (Cohen 1971, 212).

How credible, then, is the decision of the selective conscientious objector not to do wrong and to have the rest of the unit carry the burden of his conscience? Walzer (1970) emphasizes that the assessment of credibility cannot be freed from the context of the soldier's past history, that is, his way of making decisions, his record of obligations, and his awareness of the consequences of the action to himself as well as to the whole society.

In general, the assessment of credibility according to Walzer's criteria is not a hard task within the Israeli military system, where the soldier is sentenced by his battalion commander. Due to the life-long connection with the unit, the soldier's record of obligation is known to the judge, and this fact stands in favor of the highly credible soldier. Quite remarkably, it is learned from the refusers' reports that, almost without any previous experience, most of the Israeli commanders followed Walzer's line of inquiry when attempting to identify the credibility of the claims presented to them by the selective conscientious objectors in their units. The refusers were aware of quest for credibility, as one of them explained:

It was hard to realize that you were no longer *part* of the *minority* of individuals who think differently but rather an *exceptional* person. Whereas the public knows how to treat the first group, it does not know how to swallow the second one. Being a refuser in this society not only means a constant need to defend your opinions but your whole character.

The refusers further knew that their record of obligation fulfillment was the key to credibility — among themselves as well as between their group and the rest of the soldiers in the IDF. As one of them asserted, "I am sure that if you would interview the rest of the refusers, you would find that only few had done as I had in military service." And another added to this:

There is one consideration that I do not accept: that others do the work because of my absence. This is not accurate. The burden of the reserves, even among the fighting units let alone among all the units, is not equally shared. I have a friend who did one hundred days of reserve service this year and I (regardless of the fact that I was in prison) was doing thirty days in Lebanon. And what about the Orthodox, or those who pretend that they are Orthodox and do not serve? . . . I am not sure that I chose the easy way when I refused: sitting in prison, the terrible dilemmas before, and the fact that people point a finger at you and do not want to talk to you is not simple at all.

The desire to preserve one's own credibility often marked the gap between the fighting reservists and the career combatants, as is reflected in the words of this refuser, who is concerned about the potential credibility of his moral claims:

The law in the IDF allows me to refuse to obey an illegal command. Apparently this is a very clear and indeed highly moral rule of which I am proud. But in the reality of war, this is a very complicated issue and does not respond to practical morality but rather to the abstract. Let me give you an example of how meaningless this rule is: let's imagine that I am commanded or instructed to "purify" to "ventilize" or whatever nice army jargon word (which I did not endorse) to "select" the terrorists from the civilian population — and let us imagine that a few armed men and women would come out from a hospital building and my commander would instruct me to kill all of them — and I refuse! You have to see the entire scenario — I am in a middle of *war* — if I refuse it might cost me my life and other people's lives (needless to talk about the punishment for refusal under fire) . . . and the situation is very pressing. Let us assume that I refuse to perform this order. The trial would take place many months after this case when everybody would be much smarter about the justice of the war, as more information would exist. The best I would be able to do is to present the event in an abstract way — never with its enormous complexity and practical tension. You have to understand, when I joined the mission I automatically made some compromises concerning my morality since the rules of the games *there* are different from the rules of the game when you are an outsider — not in terms of justice but in terms of your ability to practice principles in which you believe when you are an outsider. The paradox is that the colonel, who would sentence me for doing the wrong acts in the battlefield, is most likely the one who has never been there, and the one who has no commitment to the reserve soldier but rather to the career officers above him who hold his promotion in their hands. By becoming a selective conscientious objector, *I prevent myself from being forced into a situation in which it would be inevitable that I would have to carry out illegal commands.*

The refusers in this sample often contrasted their claim for credibility with the demands of the individual soldier in some prestigious units in the IDF (with their prestigious record of obligation fulfillment). In the words of the refusers, these units (most notably the paratroopers) did not "allow" themselves to have many refusers as it might have raised questions regarding the credibility of the entire unit. In such units, even though the potential refuser might have held morally motivated arguments, his action was regarded as an a priori "political" and/or noncredible one, and he was very often denied the "privilege" of being imprisoned. Most illustrating is the story of an entire paratroop brigade repeatedly called to service from the first day of the war, which eventually was not happy about its assigned mission during the morally controversial blockade of Beirut.

Due to the slow process of recruiting utilized, this brigade had been negatively labeled by the minister of defense (a former paratrooper himself) as the "brigade which was not recruited" (after deciding to dismiss the entire brigade from the reserves). Soldiers who belonged to fighting units, in particular, viewed this move as a cynical one, because it indicated that soldiers not serving at all or whose units are not called for duty, are more morally credible since they are not lacking motivation.

The following is the story of a paratrooper refuser from this brigade, a doctoral student and a father of three children.

I have belonged to the paratroopers since my compulsory service. . . . I guess I do not have to tell you what we have done in the reserves all these years . . . for example in the Yom Kippur War I was in the reserves 192 days, for over half a year, when all my friends finished their studies without me. . . . We participated in the war in Lebanon from the beginning and immediately, after one weekend in the reserves . . . and a short while later . . . again to the reserves. . . . In the midst of the controversy of whether to capture Beirut or not. . . .

We knew that if the IDF decided to carry out this suicidal mission, of course we are the ones to be sent there. . . . The people were quite depressed particularly when realizing that the war had turned into a meaningless stay on Lebanese soil where soldiers were being killed everyday for no reason . . . but we all came to the reserves even though we were all depressed. . . . And then we were called again and the commander went to Lebanon to prepare the reserves. They were ambushed, and my former battalion commander was killed, and his deputy wounded . . . again the reserves was canceled till the IDF could get hold of new commanders. . . .

And then came the memorial evening for the battalion commander. Although I was thinking about refusal before, this was an evening that I was thinking about this step a lot. . . . I talked to the people around me telling them that I am considering refusal and they just did not understand what I was talking about. . . . it is not because they were *against* refusal, but because they did not realize that it was *possible* for them to do so. . . . Indeed, if you had met me a year before and talked about refusal, I would have laughed at you as well. . . . I was awaiting harsh responses . . . but there were some who shook my hand . . . some were negative. . . .

The trial of this paratrooper was dramatic as well:

After those months in pain, going to the trial was a relief. The judge was the wounded officer from that ambush . . . he was still on crutches. He was very busy and the trial took place only late at night. It was kind of an informal trial, more of a conversation. He said, "I do not want to put you on thirty-five days." But I said, "It is O.K." Then he said, "you may go outside and think for a few minutes." But I said, "there is no sense in this." So he filled in the form and said, "the battalion is going tomorrow, think about it till then." He tried to talk to me, but it did not work. . . . I got thirty-five days and later they dismissed me from the unit claiming I was too old, which of course was an excuse. . . . But as for myself, throughout these painful months, I was ready for greater punishment. . . .

THE INTERPLAY OF MORALITY AND CREDIBILITY

When measuring morality in line with Kohlberg's scale, there are, theoretically, four possible types of selective conscientious objectors. The easiest to identify is the soldier who is morally developed and highly credible. An example is given by this principled soldier:

The major knew me very well. He knew that I did not want to go to Lebanon for moral reasons and that I was willing to pay the price. . . . He was willing to release me since he knew that I was a dedicated soldier, but the problem was that he had other soldiers as well: *How would he know that those who are refusing after me indeed do it out of moral reasons?* . . . and this is

indeed a very hard question and I really understood him. So I sent him a
letter. He opened it and said, "O.K. I will release you." This is what he
thought about me as an individual. But I knew that he was also a battalion commander and he had hundreds more people under his command,
and there was no way to hide it when he was asked where I was. . . .
When he faced all of the constraints, he decided that he could not prefer
me over the others and that he could not give up in my case, though I
knew that he wanted to respond to my request very much . . . there
might be a possibility that all the battalion would refuse and he would
have to believe that they were sincere and he would pay with his position.
. . . Finally, instead of forty days in prison he gave me 14. . . .

Equally easy to identify is the one who is low in moral development and low in credibility. When a transitional 2/3 stage refuser
was asked at the end of the interview why he had not lowered his
medical profile if he did not want to go to Lebanon, he replied, "I
tried [to lower my medical profile] but I did not succeed so I
decided to refuse."

It is less clear how to identify the morally developed person with
low credibility (the one who may be articulate but is far from being
genuine) and the least morally developed person with high credibility (the soldier who is not articulate and cannot convey his
moral reasoning verbally). For the Israeli commanders it was relatively clear; due to the apolitical nature of the IDF, they tend to
define the articulate "political" refusers as falling within the category of morally superior refusers with low credibility. The three
soldiers in this sample who defined themselves as active members
of the Communist party fell into this category.

The least verbally articulate (and most often also of low socioeconomic background) but "good soldiers" with record of participation in previous fighting were more frequently found in the
category of high credibility and low stage of development. Here is
the reasoning of a credible soldier with a low level of moral development: "I told my battalion commander, 'I do not want to go to
Ansar—it is more dangerous to serve there than to sit in an IDF
prison. In the Israeli prison it is more pleasant—at least I am *inside*
and do not have to guard from outside.'"

In general, those who were identified as credible were most
often sentenced by the immediate commanders. If identified as
morally motivated, they received the minimum punishment. Those

who were not identified as credible, and/or were sensed to be politically motivated (in line with Cohen's 1971 categories), were often sent by their commanders to a higher level of command and often received the full punishment.

CREDIBILITY AND FEAR

There is nothing more natural than fear in times of war. It might become the major obstacle for a soldier in fulfilling his obligation to fight, particularly during war time, though fear is a natural feeling for every soldier and obviously not exclusive to the refusers. Perhaps it is more accurate to refer to the conscious or unconscious willingness or ability to overcome it:

I guess that if there was no punishment, many more people would have refused to go to Lebanon. When I was drafted, there was a man who shouted "I do not want to come back in a coffin." We should not be ashamed of the fact that we are afraid even of the most just war. However, there are more chances to overcome this fear when the war is just, but here we could not, at least I could not.

The refusers' inability to overcome fear was most often associated with one or more of the following factors: detachment from the unit, a military role (such as the medics, see Chapter 6), ideological positions, being new immigrants from countries without democratic regimes, being new in the unit, being from a low socioeconomic background in a unit with predominantly high socioeconomic backgrounds, subjective feelings of loneliness, and so on. However, the inability to overcome fear might be equally related to the unjust nature of the war as subjectively perceived by the soldier.

How do we know if refusal is not a cover for fear? In some cases, the commander would try to check this when attempting to find a tactical solution to the fear:

Before the trial the commander invited me to talk with him. I told him that the war is unjust and is a big mistake and that I am not going to Lebanon and finally that I do not want to die. He told me that if the reason was fear then we could both cope with it, and that he would put me in a bunker where I would not have to go out and fight. I think there is something in what he said. When I came to think about it, I realized that it was indeed fear that prevented me from going to Lebanon. It was not the fear of dying but the *unwillingness* to die for an unjust war. . . . I think I did not want to die for Arik Sharon [the Minister of Defense].

Another soldier, whose commander wanted to verify whether he was afraid or not, instructed him to talk with a psychologist in Lebanon prior to their discussion on release. The soldier refused:

Lebanon became such a scary area that the commander probably first wanted to make sure that a soldier like me would be able to step on this soil, maybe later he would change his mind. I told my commander that there are many psychologists in the Green Line and that if he needs to send me to a psychologist, I can do it here.

Though the commanders tried to avoid sentencing, when they finally did pass sentence, they "did not make it easy," as dictated by Walzer (1970). This refuser explains:

The trial was the critical moment for me, I almost gave up. . . . You're given the feeling that you are a traitor and deserter of your country and that there is a war and that you come in the middle and say that you are not going in. . . . It is a very hard feeling but I am glad that I did not surrender to it. . . . The lieutenant colonel who sentenced me twice offered me the opportunity to withdraw my decision to refuse. But I was stubborn and at the end he said that he was sorry that he had to jail me. . . . He gave me an attitude of understanding. . . . The fact is that he did not use all his legitimate power in sentencing me to thirty-five days and gave me twenty-eight. . . . Maybe he felt that there is something in what I said.

It is not surprising that both the army and the politicians had an interest in keeping the number of refusers low. It was also the concern of the unit commanders who, in addition to all the malfunctioning of the IDF and their own moral dilemmas with the war, could allow themselves neither the "luxury" of having many refusers in their unit nor of losing such a moral asset as a credible, highly moral soldier.

Under the threat of repeated jailing, some refusers considered substituting the protest with cheating the system, most notably by lowering their medical profile. Others decided simply to go, saying "I have made my protest, now I have to do what is good for me."

CREDIBILITY AND PUNISHMENT

Obviously, when compared to other countries, the punishment inflicted on the Israeli refusers was mild. However, when judged within the Israeli context, the refusers' actual punishment was more severe.

First, in terms of finance, the refuser was not paid his monthly salary during the period in prison. With a mounting inflation of 200 percent this punishment was especially significant for those imprisoned two or three times and facing an unknown future.

Second, not all the soldiers were allowed to return to their units. Some were lowered in rank. As life-long soldiers, this was a painful step.

Third, the morally motivated soldiers were very often blamed for being politically oriented; this blame was reflected in the unfavorable way in which Israeli society treated the emergence of "refusal."

Fourth, the blurred distinction between military and civilian life served as a source of punishment as well. Thus, for example, in Israeli society, decisions to hire civilians are often based on the applicant's military record. Therefore, commanders in most cases — at least in cases involving morally motivated soldiers — attempted to avoid sentencing, thereby preventing the imposition of a stigma. One refuser explains:

The commander offered me a compromise which I personally found really humiliating: that I would come with the unit to Lebanon, so I would not have the stigma of a refuser, assuming that I would not be called next time — a kind of agreement between me and the major. . . . This was very easy because it solved the problem. Now when I come to my battalion, I come as a refuser with a stigma, but when I go to Lebanon, it is forgotten both in the army and in my place of work. By using this procedure the commander probably hoped to solve a small problem for me and a big problem for the rest of the people . . . but I was not ready for this compromise . . . the problem cannot be swept under the carpet . . . things stand and fall on this issue.

Since the phenomenon was new, there were commanders who did not sense the morally motivated refusers, but like the public, categorized all of them as a priori politically motivated. Those commanders, did not seek a respectful punishment. In a rare case, a dedicated soldier in a fighting unit who decided to refuse not only received the full term of imprisonment but was hindered by his commander who objected to the civil authorities when the refuser was chosen to be an Israeli representative in the U.S. Jewish community. He did not get the job.

Interestingly enough, the stigma of refusing to serve, (particularly without the record of previous service in Lebanon) was not only an obstacle between the refusers and the society but also among the refusers themselves. One of them explained, "I thought that those who refused and belong to Yesh Gvul (see Chapter 2) are a bunch of communists, anti-Zionists and stubborn people and I had a fear of being included among them if I refused. . . . It was quite a dilemma."

Realizing the potential general reaction to an individual action, one refuser summed up the consequences of his actions thus:

Now I understand why I did not run to become a refuser—in order to translate the thoughts of objections into actions—it is not only that the action itself is hard to execute but it is also the fact that refusal is like a stone that you throw into the water: it obviously makes waves, and you can never predict if it would or would not turn into a storm that you did not expect . . . and there are many negative implications of this action . . . if, for example, there is a war with Syria. . . . You have to take all these into consideration.

CREDIBILITY AND MOTIVATION

Given the fact that the IDF is mainly a reserve army, the issue of motivation is crucial. The fact that a large majority of refusers were previously motivated soldiers (i.e., most likely credible) was quite confusing for those commanders who did not want to dismiss them for holding political ideas. Dedicated soldiers were, most often, reluctant to consider refusal during the war itself and they attempted to try to fight for their principles while inside the unit. One refuser who had fought four wars (and even had returned voluntarily to one of them while studying abroad) tells about his fight for justice inside the unit:

I was in the reserves before the war started. We all knew that there was going to be a war. . . . I felt bad about it, but somehow I let myself be swept along. I was in the column that went in on the first day. I can only recall the feeling of indescribable power, of long columns of tanks and armored cars. . . . It was not my first war, but in the beginning I had no time to think and only when we stopped in Beirut did I have my first breathing space. . . . Our unit had been together a long time under fire . . . when the first armored car stopped it all came out. There were terrible arguments among the men even inside our armored vehicle. Then I did not think of refusal. I felt that I and a few others served as a sort of brake. At least we drank from tin cans and not from the copperware from the luxurious Lebanese villas. Perhaps that is my only excuse for not refusing right then.

Several morally oriented refusers (in line with Cohen's categories), who tried to make changes from within the system, did not want to publicize their names. One of them explains, "The truth of the matter is that I was scared to refuse then, not because of what they would do to me, but because of the hue and cry it would cause, afraid of becoming the center of something." Another dedicated soldier explains how the fight for justice goes along with his motivation to serve:

I am not one of those who went to the war as a "cog in the machine." I was not happy about this war, but I could not reach a balanced conclusion at the beginning of it. . . . It was so confusing. You are called in the middle of the night . . . your animal instincts are raised . . . I was driving all night to Lebanon. . . . Maybe it is a cynical way of recruiting so you will not see the turmoils of the battle. . . . It was hard to be wise . . . after all, if it had been a war with Syria I would have gone!

Some were discouraged by the punishment, as they hoped to be protected by the law:

It is obviously true that we have to keep the law, but the prime question is "which law do we violate?" . . . On the whole I believe that even refusers are not taking the word "conscience" for granted but rather painfully try to clarify it vis à vis the actions they are required to do. If the IDF would take the issue of conscience into account, the punishment could have been avoided — it is quite ridiculous that only when a person transgresses, i.e.,

refuses to go, that his conscience is being taken into consideration. . . .
Why not to do it ahead of time?

In a way the performance of the action also marks a general
crisis in the soldiers' motivation: "I was surprised to realize when I
came out of prison that most of the people did not care what was
going on in the country . . . around them . . . I was shocked.
. . . I thought that I *would change the world but I did not.*"

There was also an overall disappointment in the justice/credibil-
ity scale of the IDF as it revealed itself in the prisons, as explained
by this credible refuser:

Even though I was at peace with myself about prison, it was very hard on
me — I was alone and had a hard time being humiliated. The worse thing
was to be equated with another prisoner who had smuggled a video from
Lebanon — the one who "got" only two weeks for this law breaking — it
made me sad that I received twenty-eight days not because of the length
of the prison time but because of the fact that my action was considered a
worse offense by the army.

Though most of the refusers did not enjoy the prison term, they
were able to acknowledge the fact that it was a mild punishment
(when the related punishments are not counted), which enabled
them to act upon their principles and remain dedicated soldiers:

I am glad that the punishment was as mild as it was. First, it showed me
the moral strength of the IDF who were not scared of a wave of refusers in
spite of this low threat. Second, it made me act upon my moral principles.
I guess that if the punishment was more severe, I would do what I could
to cheat the army and avoid service and not be punished.

Another benefit of the mild punishment is noted by the following account:

I think that it is quite dangerous to go to prison and I wonder if all the
refusers thought about it ahead of time. You are going to sit among
military law breakers and this is a defined company. Throughout my time
as an officer in the artillery, these were many of my soldiers, whom I tried
to help, etc., and now I was sitting with them since I was also fighting in
jail the IDF, a fight which I chose to do, and they also had a fight with
the IDF, and suddenly I found myself supporting any deserter, etc. I

am afraid to think how we would all support these people if the stay in prison was longer.

In general, the prison experience was not detached from the refuser's entire moral dilemma, as noted by this refuser: "The physical action of stepping inside prison is the hardest part: it is both the symbol and the reality of your action. You do not know what there is behind this door, even if you think you know."

In concluding this chapter, it would be fair to comment that at least within the Israeli reality of war, selective conscientious objection should be regarded as more credible than the conscientious objectors who often take advantage of the social system rather than pointing out some weak points in the system that they are ready to serve and correct.

The following credible refuser's comment sums up the issue of credibility as a selective conscientious objector: "I do not regret my action, although it caused me a lot of pain. I *used* the army *against* the army since I am *for* the army."

NOTES

1. At the time of editing the manuscript (September 1988) a group of army officers and high ranking physicians are being blamed for releasing reservists from service with faked medical evidence.

2. Reservists always contributed physically and morally in times of military crisis even more than expected. For example, during the War of Attrition, voluntary soldiers calling themselves "the tigers" joined units stationed on the Suez canal to help them. During the uprising in the territories these days, reservists up to the rank of major joined units of regular compulsory service soldiers stationed in the West Bank in order "to be with them in the hard moments" (Linn, in preparation).

Selective Conscientious Objection: An Action of Justice or Care?

The view of the moral actor as a free agent, capable of rising above the circumstances of his or her environment by virtue of moral principles, has been central both to ethical theory and to psychological research on moral development. As described by Kohlberg (1976, 35), the ideal moral actor adopts a "prior to society" or "postconventional" standpoint from which he "is aware of the values and rights prior to the social attachments and contracts." From this vantage point, Kohlberg's thesis implies that the moral actor is able to choose between conflicting rights and duties without any personal and societal constraints. This individualistic outlook is the hallmark of moral autonomy and moral maturity.

Most people are portrayed as "conventional" moral thinkers (stages 3 and 4) in Kohlberg's terms and are susceptible to personal and situational influences upon their actions. Moral actors who manifest "postconventional" thinking (stages 5 and 6) are rarely found in studies of moral development (Lickona 1980), and under the pressure of circumstances often tend to "lower" their mode of functioning, either out of a "realistic appraisal of the situation" (Locke 1983a, 166) or simply out of a "calculated restructuring of the informational and social fields" (Milgram 1974, 7). This change of moral perception, particularly the disparity between hypothetical judgment and actual behavior, was not considered as limiting the explanatory power of the moral theory per se (Broughton

1978) but instead has been ascribed to the unfortunate intervention of such "nonmoral" factors as "ego strength" (Krebs 1967).

Over the past two decades, experimental evidence of moral autonomy has come from a limited range of action situations, where
people who are strangers to one another are asked to return questionnaires (Krebs and Rosenwald 1977), not to cheat on tests
(Kohlberg 1984), to help others unknown to them (McNamee
1978). Though Kohlberg and Candee (1984) claimed that "in the
clear majority of studies using Kohlberg's measure of moral reasoning, there is a correlation between relatively high moral judgment and what is commonly considered to be moral behavior
including honesty, resistance to temptation, and altruism" (p. 52),
the most common type of dilemma situation examined was that of
"resistance to temptation." In these situations, the right action is
conceptualized as *not acting*, that is, as refraining from acting in
one's presumed self-interest (not bothering to return the questionnaires, cheating on the test, not helping others). Thus conceived,
moral action (i.e., nonaction) depends on the ability to resist the
temptation to act spontaneously or unreflectively. For right action,
in this view, *hesitation* is an inevitable prerequisite.

Consequently, from a developmental standpoint, moral action
has been premised on the intervention of reason between the child
(tempted to act on his or her impulses) and the society (which
demands or holds up an ideal of restraint or consideration for
others). Thus for the child to act morally, he or she must rely on
the intervention of reason, which "causes man . . . to HESITATE
in his interaction with the milieu" (Langer 1969, 14). In this view,
the more elaborated the form of reasoning, the more central the
role of hesitation in moral functioning. Locke (1981, 177), for
example, notes that "the more sophisticated our moral understanding, the more difficult it may be to resolve conflicting moral
claims."

Obviously "when the (moral) dilemma is prearranged so that
only *one* of the two opposed actions can be judged as right"
(Kohlberg and Candee, 1984, 62), the moral actor is required to
be obsessed with singling out the most just claim of right. This
prearrangement negates the possibility of viewing the moral conflict as unresolvable. In this chapter, I address the tension between
moral action premised on detachment (resolving conflicting

claims) and moral action grounded in connection (facing conflicts of loyalties).

The conception of the highly moral actor and the right moral action as premised on detachment might be illustrated in the case of Michael Bernhardt, the only soldier who claimed not to take part in the massacre in My Lai.[1] Kohlberg praises Bernhardt for *not acting*, that is, not shooting. He views this "action" (i.e., not shooting) as consistent with his principled moral competence and judgment reasoning of the My Lai situation (Kohlberg 1984). To Kohlberg, Bernhardt exemplifies moral action; as a moral actor, he is capable of seeing the ultimate priority of human life and of valuing life irrespective of societal categories (Vietnamese/Americans) or constraints.

Kohlberg's description of Bernhardt implies that his action is the most just or most moral course of action; that in the situation he faces, *not shooting* is the morally principled resolution to the moral dilemma posed. Yet, there are other ways to think about what constitutes moral action in these circumstances or what characterizes the highly moral person acting under these constraints. An example of such an alternative moral position at My Lai is provided by Thompson, who rescued nine Vietnamese by threatening Calley (Hersh 1970). In contrast to Bernhardt's *passive* fulfillment of moral principles (setting the highest priority on life, treating persons as ends rather than as means, upholding moral principles at the cost of disobeying authority and so forth), Thompson *initiated spontaneously* an *active* action of help to the people he was facing, who were in need. He did so by attending to the parameters of the situation (the threat posed by Calley) and by inventing an effective response (threatening Calley so that he would not bother him while he was taking survivors from the ditches). Thompson's action implies discerning that Calley might respond to threat, discovering a way of threatening Calley that was effective, drawing on knowledge of Calley, the situation, and of his relationship with Calley (as well as perhaps knowledge of himself and of what actions he was capable of taking).

The contrast between Bernhardt and Thompson is heightened by the fact that though considered a principled, moral thinker, Bernhardt was not the first (if at all) to report the immoral action to the authorities (Hersh 1970). Though Bernhardt's moral reasoning, as assessed by Kohlberg, reflects a capacity for postconventional moral judgment (a high level of moral development) this *nonaction* of *not reporting* might be judged as a manifestation of indifference, or lack of concern for the others around him. This reading is supported by the fact that the injustice of My Lai was revealed only accidently after a long period of silence (Hersh 1970). Bernhardt seems to be consistent not only in his principles but also in taking a moral stand of *nonaction*. As he explained to Kohlberg: "When I thought of shooting people I figured: "well, I am going to be doing *my own war*, let them do their own war" (Kohlberg 1984, 549, emphasis added).

Whether there is more than one moral voice within each person and whether different moral voices may prevail in certain situations are age-old questions. Moral thinkers such as, for example, the biblical interpreters, also questioned what moral actions were deemed praiseworthy and what characterizes the highly moral or righteous person. Looking for an example of a highly moral actor, they refer to the case of Noah whom God ordered to build an ark to save his family and the family of animals before the flood covered the earth to destroy the evil. The Bible testifies: "Noah was in his generations a man of righteous and whole hearted. Noah walked with God" (Genesis 6:9).

Some sages explain this praise as being a righteous in *his* generation, meaning his evil generation. Others interpret this characterization of Noah as indirect criticism. Had Noah lived in Abraham's time, he would have been insignificant (Slotowitz 1975). Noah, these sages explain, was content to build an ark to save only himself and did not intercede on behalf of his generation but let them perish. Abraham, in contrast, did intercede on behalf of others. In essence, Abraham questioned the view of himself or his people as the only righteous ones by pleading to God not to destroy the city of Sodom: "Oh, let not the Lord be angry, and I will speak yet but this once. Peradventure ten shall be found there" (Genesis 18:32).

The story of Abraham's action on behalf of Sodom, in contrast to Noah's *nonaction* on behalf of those slated to drown in the flood, suggests that the moral actor or highly moral person is one who actively searches for possible moral resolutions within the dilemma situation, rather than simply refraining from taking action that is inconsistent with righteousness of moral principles. The realization of a different mode of moral action implies a change in moral psychology research.

The dimensions of attachment and detachment within the dilemma situation in addition to the dimensions of justice and injustice thus become a focus for moral concern. The moral voices of justice and care have been distinguished in terms of this shift in the focus of attention, with the voice of justice identified by the articulation of concerns about equality and reciprocity and the voice of care, identified by the articulation of concerns about connection and response (Gilligan 1982b). These two voices imply different ways of conceptualizing moral action or what actions are worthy of praise or blame (see also Gilligan 1986a,b; Gilligan and Wiggins 1987).

That biblical interpreters were troubled by the way in which Noah *detaches* himself from the dilemma situation and solves it as an outsider (from the vantage point of Noah's ark), suggests that concerns about detachment have a long history in the Western tradition. Their criticism of Noah as lacking in care, the view of his righteousness as compromised by his willingness to turn away from others—to separate himself from them, indicates that concerns about attachment and about care are persistent human concerns.

Contemporary psychological research indicates that both women and men tend to introduce concerns about both justice and care when discussing moral conflicts they have faced. They also tend to focus on one set of concerns or to render either justice or care considerations more pressing or more salient (see Gilligan and Wiggins 1987; Brown, et al. 1987).

Furthermore, although women and men raise justice and care concerns in discussing moral conflicts and thus identify both as moral concerns, a focus on care concerns was demonstrated almost exclusively by women among educationally advantaged North American adults and adolescents. Adolescent and adult males in this population were more likely to focus on justice considerations in resolving moral conflicts, and thus they best illustrate Kohlberg's conception of morality as justice (honoring rights, fulfilling duties, acting in accordance with the principle of equal respect, etc.).

Within this justice framework, the care focus in women's moral thinking initially appeared as a "different voice" (Gilligan 1982a),

a voice characterized by concerns about connection and disconnection. From this "care perspective," disconnection or detachment
create the conditions for carelessness or neglect as well as for
ignorance, for not knowing either what is happening or how to
respond. A care voice was characterized not only by a different
way of approaching, experiencing or imagining relationships (as
webs of connection rather than as hierarchies of inequality or
balanced scales) but also by a different way of experiencing and
conceiving oneself in relation to others, as connected and therefore
interdependent (attached) rather than as separate and therefore
capable of objectivity (and objectification).

A powerful image of a connected sense of self is provided by
Martin Luther King (1964) when he says in the letter from Bir-
mingham jail: "We are caught in an inescapable network of mutu-
ality, tied in a single garment of destiny. Whatever affects one
directly, affects all indirectly" (p. 79).

Only the word *caught* suggests the negative valuation commonly
placed on relationships of dependence within American society
(with its valuing of independence) or the uneasiness about connection or attachment (which from a psychological vantage point
appears to be more characteristic of males). The tie between conceptions of self and conceptions of morality (see Gilligan 1977,
1982b) is grounded in the fact that it is only through connection
with others that one is able to see or hear others in their own
terms. The difference between taking another's point of view (or
speaking another's language) and putting *oneself* in the other person's shoes is the same as the difference between a sense of oneself
as connected with others (their words entering one's ears, their
images on one's retina, the culture entering via language, etc.) and
a sense of oneself as separate and bounded, marked off from others
by a psychic membrane that is regarded, ideally, as impermeable
(the autonomous self of Kohlberg's principled stages).

One criticism that has been made against the "different voice"
approach to moral development is that the language of care per-
tains to different kinds of relationships characterized by Kohlberg
as "personal" or "particular" (i.e., limited by time, place, and context). Care reasoning thus is seen as desirable in the private realm
but undesirable or inapplicable in the public sphere. Women's
proficiency in care reasoning has been linked, on this basis, with

women's exclusion from the public domain, an exclusion also considered responsible for limiting women's moral development. Sichel (1985), echoing these criticisms, asks in effect how moral actors in public life could reason in terms of care. She questions whether a care-oriented moral voice could provide an adequate basis for resolving public domain moral dilemmas. In response to such questions I turn to the data on Israeli selective conscientious objectors, data that offer an empirical basis for thinking through these theoretical questions.

THE MORAL VOICE OF THE SELECTIVE CONSCIENTIOUS OBJECTORS

Loyalty to the members of the unit is a familiar universal phenomenon within armies and throughout wars (Hoffman 1981; Marshal 1978), yet within the Israeli context it holds another dimension: the lifelong connection with friends within a civilian as well as a military context (Gal 1986) and the central part of the army experience in the formation of the Israeli males' identity. This identity is socially constructed and joins two lines of social and moral development; the morality of obligation and duties and the morality of belonging (attachment) and loyalty.

The refusers' primary focus on taking an objective and legal view of their own actions (stage 4) and attesting to the individual's right to exclude himself from morally conflicting situations (stages 4/5, 5) is similar to the logic Kohlberg traced in the case of Bernhardt. The language used is often identical, exemplifying the stark separation of self ("my war," "my problem") and other ("their war"). One Israeli refuser presents it this way:

I think that in the refusal I succeeded in solving *my own problem about the war*. I am not sure if the way that I chose is 100 percent the right way, but I am sure that this is the right way for me. This was not my war . . . I let them fight *their own war* . . . [emphasis added]

Moreover, as was claimed by the refusers, only by *not going* to Lebanon could they succeed in preserving their moral integrity. This notion of a single, most moral solution to the war dilemma was consonant with the consistency of their reasoning across different Kohlberg stages and between different dilemma contexts (Linn 1985).

One of the most visible characteristics of this *"nonaction"* (not going) is the lonely manner in which the act was constructed and executed. All reported on loose connections and detachment from the unit, some because they felt they were holding different and uncompromised moral principles, some had no friends in the unit, and some were transferred from one unit to the other due to their military role (such as the medics). Other refusers, though having a unit of their own, did not consider themselves as attached to it, due either to their extreme ideological stand or to the fact that the Lebanon war was their first reserve service with their unit.

I did not have any special connection with my unit. The Lebanon war was my first reserve service with this unit after my regular service . . . As I spent some time until the trial staying with the people who were packing to go to Lebanon, I began to know the people, and it became extremely hard to refuse . . . You feel some kind of commitment . . . I really don't know how to explain this feeling . . . You feel that you are surrounded by people . . . then the commander came and tried to inspire me, and you feel that you are swept along, pulled by the power of the people, but then I decided that I did not want to be swept along by these people and at this stage I decided to remove myself. It is so easy to go along with the whole crowd . . . though these people did not want to go to Lebanon, being together gave them some unconscious excitement . . . and you really need inner fortitude to resist it.

For some, refusal matched their tendency to adopt detachment or self-control as a mode of resolution for personal, moral dilemmas (see p. 57).

And for others, the action of refusal came as a surprise — not believing in their ability to act as they did:

In the case of refusal, you first feel that you have no option but to act in a certain way. It is a very strong feeling and you cannot sit calmly unless you do it. Only then, one's moral thoughts become clear.

Thus the ability to perform *this* type of action as refusal seems to have been shaped by some contextual factors (such as detachment from the unit) as well as the intervention of personality "nonmoral factors" such as the courage to be alone (Fromm 1981).

Maybe more than any other action, selective conscientious objection may best serve to illuminate the one-dimensional way in which Kohlberg's theory has been utilized in the examination of real life moral actions. It is no longer a secret that measures of moral reasoning were found to be highly correlated with distinct political orientations (Candee 1976). Moreover, postconventional (and detached!) thinking has been found to be more associated with political actions that were oriented toward *rejection* of the adequacy of the system's conventional definitions than other types of real life actions (Emler et al. 1983). Within the Israeli context, the refusers' action symbolizes a strong rejection of a traditional and historically respected norm of collective struggles for survival, combined with a readiness for self-sacrifice for principles of justice.

Examination of the sample of refusers in line with Lyons' procedure (1982) as refined by Gilligan and Attanucci (1988), indicates that 66 percent of the refusers demonstrated a predominantly justice focus in their reasoning about their refusal; 10 percent demonstrated a care focus; and 24 percent elaborated both sets of concerns. The 66 percent who focused on justice considerations were not necessarily principled moral thinkers according to Kohlberg's developmental criteria (Linn 1985). Furthermore, it is important to point out that even in the group of justice-focused refusers, the voice of *care* can be identified, though it is not the dominant one.

Prior to the war I was already an outsider in my unit. I had many verbal clashes with the other soldiers in terms of ideology and government policy. I knew that at least on the hypothetical level I was completely detached from the others . . . *but the real problem was the actual detachment* — that you are refusing and going to prison. The same bus that took me to the prison continued with them to Lebanon. I *felt very bad that they would feel cold and I would be warm in prison*, but the dominant feeling was that I was not part of them anyhow. [emphasis added to identify care considerations]

Moreover, according to their descriptions of their decisions, the voice of care rather than justice principles motivated 28 out of 36 refusers (78 percent) to insist on returning to their units upon their release from prison. The morality of justice appears to go hand in

hand with the morality of care where genuine dilemmas or unresolvable moral conflict are described.

After prison I had the option not to return to my unit, but then I decided
I should go back: I am still thinking that there are real survival problems
for our country and that there might be times where the existence of
Israel would be in danger and a strong army is necessary. I feel that *I still
have a problem with this and I cannot get rid of the feeling that it is difficult to be freed
from this dilemma.* [emphasis added]

Whereas the physical, ideological, or personal detachment was
seen by the refusers as based on their moral principles (Linn
1989a), they nevertheless viewed detachment as unfortunate and
in some sense not moral. The desire to be attached to or *included* in
the unit both in recognition of a common or shared future and for
the sake of their moral integrity in relation to others is reflected in
the constant tension between duties and loyalties. For the Israeli
soldier, the dilemma of refusal marks this dilemma of moral development.

The worst parts of the refusal were going to the commander, going to the
unit, and coping with the prison . . . I am really attached to the unit, the
people, the commander, and the commander persuaded me not to refuse.
He did not want to put me in jail . . . The commander is really my
friend . . . we went through the same hard times during the Yom Kippur
War . . . and other campaigns and suddenly you find yourself on the
other side . . . And what happens after prison? . . . You come back to
serve with the same people and you still believe that if Syria attacks us
tomorrow, you should go with them to fight, to protect your country
without hesitation . . . How would they accept you?

Most striking is the care consideration presented to the refusers
by their fighting commanders who were obliged to sentence them,
yet recognized their sense of justice as an asset to the entire unit
and therefore did not want to dismiss them. The highly moral and
highly credible soldier from Chapter 7 explains:

Five minutes before the brigade was about to go to Lebanon and everybody was on the bus—the major told me, "Now you stay by yourself for
five minutes, without anyone and you make the final decision, and you

have to know that after this I will have to sentence you." I told him, "I do not need this five minutes, I am not going with you and that is that. I don't need even one second." But he said, "No! You will think for another five minutes," . . . and I guess he was right from his point of view, because even though my thoughts were consolidated by this time, this was a very hard process . . . those five minutes seemed to be forever. . . . I guess he wanted to be at peace with himself that he had done all that he could in order to convince me to go to Lebanon. . . . I will appreciate it for the rest of my life . . . and this is one of the major reasons that I did not want to leave the battalion. . . . After prison he phoned me at home and asked me how I was feeling.

In terms of Kohlberg's theory, many of these refusers qualify as highly moral actors despite the fact that their comrades had to assume extra burdens when serving with fewer people in the unit. The morality of their action was characterized by the extent to which their high degree of hesitation in joining the group action enabled them to preserve their moral integrity passively in their own constructed justice ark. But even then, the refusers were not at peace with their consciences until they proved to themselves, and particularly to their society, that their action was motivated by concerns about connection and care as well as by justice reasoning. Many would want to be viewed as moral actors who emphasized the dilemma that is still there, even after the performance of the action (see Gilligan 1982a,b) — the one for whom the moral solution is not linear, but rather spiral; the one to whom the morality of the situation is not as clear as a formal logic of moral reasoning might have promised; the one who realizes that his friends in his unit had assumed the burden of his conscience:

You ask me now at the end of the interview if there is a question regarding the refusers that you should have asked but did not . . . Yes, I believe that you did not touch upon all the hypothetical situations that left us in a dilemma . . . O.K. We have refused, we did not want to participate in these military operations . . . and we thought that if everybody would do the same, things would be much better . . . However, an immediate withdrawal now would be a disaster both for the Palestinians as well as for the Israeli citizens in the border areas. Thus, we have an unsolved dilemma . . . *I think we cannot bear only a morality of conscience . . . There is also a morality of responsibility.* [emphasis added]

For the Israeli refuser, both moralities cannot be exercised and evaluated apart from social relationships, as explained by this soldier:

I am close to 40 years old and I have taken part in all the wars since I was 18 years old . . . I could easily be transferred to a unit where I could serve in an office and not on the battlefield . . . I am not going to do so since I feel that it would be an escape to close my eyes and say to myself — I am O.K. I got out . . . This is wrong because in this way I solve *my problem* and I let my friends in the unit do the work. I want to return to my unit upon release from prison since if I continue to serve and remain *part* of the unit, I buy myself the right to criticize and the right to shout . . .

CONCLUSION

The development of the mature moral actor might be seen as following two paths, not necessarily mirroring one another: the course of justice and the course of care. These two paths differ not only in their moral categories but also in their emotional components: the hesitation, passivity, and impartiality in the justice path, and spontaneity, activity, and involvement in the care path. These modes of understanding are as ancient as the biblical moral heroes. They seem to stand in different relationships to the emotional dimension of moral action. In the case of Noah, emotions seem not to be a crucial component of the just or righteous action.

God had many ways of saving Noah. Why then did he trouble Noah with this building (an ark)? So that the generation of the flood would see Noah occupying himself with it for one hundred and twenty years and ask him: "What are you doing" and Noah would answer them: "God is about to bring a flood on the world." Then perhaps the people would repent. (Pearl 1970, 34)

However, in the case of Abraham, an action guided by the logic of care entails an emotional dimension, a feeling of connection or involvement in the fate of others:

Abraham "stands *before* God to plead for the lives of Pagans of another race; Pagans, what is more, who were to become the eternal symbol of human depravity. He neither rejoices at the dawn of the evil, nor adopts an attitude of *indifference*. He feels a sense of kinship with those human beings of Sodom, and a sense of *involvement* in their fate" (Sarna 1966, 143, emphasis added).

Obviously, Abraham is still in a dilemma though the crisis is over. The question that remains and that seems applicable in the case of selective conscientious objectors in Israel today is how to maintain or create connections with others in the face of differences with them.

This developmental question is not addressed by Kohlberg's theory. Kohlberg's morality of justice does not provide multiple paths of action possibilities but rather implies one right way — being just, most often by stepping outside the system, that is by separation and detachment (Linn 1989a). But as already noted by Hare (1981), who refers to the Israeli-Palestinian relationships as an example of moral conflict, there are true moral dilemmas that have *no just solution*. Many real life dilemmas throughout the life cycle have no just or righteous solution, no most moral or single path of action. Selective conscientious objection in Israel is one of them. Indeed, "prior to society" evaluation, that is, the possibility to "get out," is a luxurious outlook that few are capable of doing according to current data (Blasi 1980, 1983; Kohlberg 1984) and that even if possible is not always considered moral by those who do it.

When analyzing the ways in which individuals resolve real life dilemmas, it is helpful to view morality as developing out of at least two basic human experiences: the experience of attachment and separation, and the experience of equality and inequality (Gilligan 1986). Imbalance between these two paths can create moral problems as illustrated by the behavior of Noah and Abraham. Noah failed despite his righteousnesses to perceive the dimension of care in that he did not even protest God's command to him to save himself, his family, and his principles while leaving others to perish. In this he resembles Bernhardt. As long as the language of moral responsibility refers only to passive fulfillment of one's own principles and does not represent the other dimension of responsiveness in relationships with others, the psychology of moral development continues to promote a flood of data that in the name of righteousness drowns the moral conflicts that often occur in real lives.

NOTE

1. Kohlberg seems not to differentiate between mature moral thoughts and credibility (see Linn 1989b). He always refers to Bernhardt as *the* only soldier who did not shoot in My Lai. However, this claim has been stated to Kohlberg, but its validity and credibility have never been questioned by him. Colonel William G. Eckhardt, JAGC, who was the chief prosecutor in the case of the senior army commander on the ground at the My Lai incident, was asked by the author about Kohlberg's claim. Eckhardt's response was "everybody was shooting in My Lai, I do not know that Bernhardt did not shoot" (personal communication, January 22, 1987, U.S. meeting, Washington, "Morality in and out of war: professional conduct on the battlefield"). Nevertheless, in this chapter I refer to Bernhardt's testimony to Kohlberg as credible.

_____ *Chapter 9* _____

When All Come Together

For the Israeli reserve soldiers who took part in this study, the Lebanon war was a direct attack on their conception of the Israeli *defense* army. When forced to fight an optional war, to control civilian population without success (having had this experience before in the occupied territories), and to decide the impossible task of differentiating between terrorists and innocent civilians they gradually and painfully started to question the meaning of their affiliation to the Israel *Defense* Forces. Since they had never pledged their commitment to an army that deviates from the pure concept of defense in their eyes, refusal was possible. Yet, they were reluctant to use this mode of action, since they felt commitment to their fellow soldiers as well as being seriously concerned about the security of the country, which might have been threatened without their knowledge.

However, when the war stretched beyond their familiar notion of time, space, and moral criteria, it generated a *split* between the army and the nation, a split that paved the way for refusal.

It started when the burden of reserve service in the extended conflict was not shared by all (*Ha'aretz* April 11, 1985), when it became "a war in another place" (*Ha'aretz* August 10, 1984), conducted in a "lost country" (*Ha'aretz* September 23, 1983), where the "IDF soldiers are stuck in the mud" (Yediot Acharonot December 28, 1984). Those who fulfilled their duty could not share their experience with all the people around them. Most notable was the discouragement of the kibbutz fighters; the traditional source of IDF officers, of whom each soldier is this society's "son":

A son comes from a war in Lebanon, and he is not welcomed by the member who might have said: "We are proud of you" but rather "Are you crazy? Haven't you got better things to do?" (*Ma'ariv* May 17, 1984).

Actually, this, the longest war in the country's history (Timmerman 1985), simply reflected Orwell's (1949) prophecy: "It would probably be accurate to say that *by becoming continuous, war has ceased to exist*" (p. 164). Though it was the first war that was brought to each Israeli citizen's living room through the TV screen, not all the citizens participated, or even cared. Dedicated soldiers reported their experience as being "the cannon fodder of the people in the rear" (*Yediot Acharonot* September 24, 1984), and for some this feeling paved the way for refusal.

We were bombing Beirut all the time. A man from the TV came after we had finished shooting. He waited and waited and nothing happened. So finally . . . he said: "If you do not shoot I am leaving — I need a program for tonight!" One of the commanders began asking permission to shoot . . . That shocked me. My commander returned that evening from leave and I told him that I would do only the minimum, no more . . . That was my first step toward refusal.

With the deteriorating economy, the army-nation split became even more visible: "My boss is a major in the army. Nevertheless, he asked us very seriously *not* to go to reserve service no matter what we do."

Finally, the split reached the army itself. There were almost two armies: the reservists who left their workplaces and served in Lebanon and those among the professional army of clerks, who recruited the reservists but never *served there* and could not even share the moral struggle of the individual refuser who was serving a long time in Lebanon prior to his decision to take this stand.

I reached my decision after a long and bitter debate with myself, after being a long time in Lebanon . . . and here I am being taken to prison by the officer, sitting in a small car and thinking all the way whether I am being fair to my comrades who are now on their way to Lebanon, and whether my action will make the right impact. I felt that for those army officers and clerks in the car who were doing their routine work of processing us (with) all the paperwork, we were just an additional burden. They could not even (know) that we refused, not out of hatred for Israel, but rather as a result of serious thought and care. But they, of course, never served in Lebanon and treat us as a burden.

Along with the refusers' subjective perception of the fading moral uniqueness of the army, there was also a feeling of their detachment from it. Refusal was but a move to prevent their deterioration into chessboard soldiers:

When the Americans were held hostage by the Iranian Ayatollah, suddenly it came to my mind that since I serve in an elite unit, I might be called to act to rescue them. Thank God, it did not happen; it was just a theoretical exercise and perhaps exemplifies the feeling of a soldier who does not want to be regarded as chess-piece soldier.

It seems that the subjective perception of detachment from Israeli society led those soldiers oriented toward justice who were predisposed to act individualistically upon their judgments to adopt the choice of refusal as the right, moral action in their eyes.

On this alienated ground, history has known many other conscientious objectors (Scheissel 1968; Gaylin 1970). Yet, for the Israeli soldier, his case is slightly different, since he is faced with two additional moral constraints prior to his personal ability to translate his objection to a specific war into the action of refusal. One is related to the daily physical threat regarding the survival of the state of Israel. Here, as already indicated by Chomski (in Blatt et al. 1975), "There is no such simple answer as the straightforward and appropriate slogan of the American resistance 'Get Out.' The resistance in Israel faces a more difficult and intellectual moral challenge." The other is the realization that the army is a necessity (Walzer 1983), and life in Israeli society means lifelong reserve service as a primary civil obligation.

Obviously, this work is awaiting further analysis with the author's existing data on those highly moral soldiers who objected to the war yet took part in it, making extra efforts and self-sacrifices in order to preserve their moral principles in the battlefield.

Israeli society is far from indicating refusal as a highly moral action. This phenomenon was not mentioned among the important events and consequences of the war in Lebanon (*Ha'aretz, Ma'ariv, Yediot Acharonot* June 7, 1985). It seems that for Israeli society selective conscientious objection during war is not yet a threat and, therefore, this topic is ignored. Is it a sign of the immaturity of this society to cope and develop morally out of this experience?

The phenomenon of selective conscientious objection is a sign of strength of Israeli democracy. On the external level, it highlights from another (and unconventional) angle the moral difference between the IDF and the Arab armies from whom we do not hear about selective conscientious objection. It further sharpens a fundamental problem within the Israeli society, which calls for a theoretical consideration: why would the conscience of the fighting soldiers be dismissed a priori from consideration, whereas the conscience of thousands who are not serving at all are recognized without any dilemma?

At the writing of this book, December 1987, during the undeclared war in the territories, three reserve soldiers were in prison for conscientious refusal. At the time of editing the manuscript, September 1988, there are over forty jailed refusers.[1] At the present time the Israeli soldiers are repeatedly called to exercise their conscience in a fight against terrorists along the Lebanese border and in pursuing a government policy against violent activities of civilians in the territories.

Unlike the era following the war in Lebanon, there seems to be a growing awareness within the Israeli public that the dilemma of becoming a selective conscientious objector is no longer the exclusive dilemma of the extremist or politically oriented soldier. Refusal seems to be one of several behavioral choices a soldier can consider and/or adopt (not necessarily the right one or the most effective one) when faced with a morally problematic situation. Certainly, it remains questionable whether it is moral to send a soldier to a war he cannot *morally* win.

It remains also a question for The Little Prince of Antoine de Saint-Exupéry.

[The prince questions the king about the nature of a just authority:]

"I should like to see a sunset . . . Do me that kindness . . . Order the sun to set . . . "

"If I ordered a general to fly from one flower to another like a butterfly, or to write a tragic drama, or to change himself into a sea bird, and if the general did not carry out the order that he had received, which one of us would be in the wrong?" the king demanded, "the general, or myself?"

"You," said the prince firmly.

"Exactly. One must require from each one the duty which each one can perform," the king went on. "Accepted authority rests first of all on reason. If you ordered your people to go and throw themselves into the sea, they would rise up in revolution. I have the right to require obedience because my orders are reasonable." (p. 36)

NOTE

1. At the present time the dedicated IDF soldier who does not evade service is sent to calm down civilian rioters in the territories; he is ordered to use tear gas, truncheons, plastic bullets, and beatings as the means of preventing and punishing the rioters. The Minister of Defense declares that he is *responsible* for this policy, which aims to harm as many of the rioters as possible. Unknowingly, the individual IDF soldier is being asked to perform flagrantly illegal commands for which *he*, not the authorities issuing the commands, is personally responsible and subject to military trial.

References

Arendt, H. (1972) Crisis in the Republic. New York: Harcourt, Brace, Jovanovich.

Aronfreed, J. (1968) Conduct and Conscience: The Socialization of Internalized Control over Behavior. New York: Academic Press.

Bandura, A. and Walters, R. H. (1963) Social Learning and Personality Development. New York: Holt.

Bem, J. D. (1970) Beliefs, Attitude and Human Affairs. Belmont CA: Brooks Cole.

Blatt, M., Davis, U., and Klinbaum, P. (1975) Dissent and Ideology in Israel: Resistance to the Draft (1948-1973). London: Ithaca Press.

Blasi, A. (1980) Bridging moral cognition and moral action: A critical review of the literature. *Psychological Bulletin*, 88:1-45.

Blasi, A. (1983) Moral cognition and moral action: A theoretical perspective. *Developmental Review*, 3:178-210.

Blasi, A. (1985) The moral personality: Reflection for social science and education. In M. Berkowitz and F. Oser (eds): Moral Education: Theory and Application (pp. 433-444). Hillsdale, NJ: Erlbaum, 147-165.

Blasi, A., and Oresick, R. J. (1986) Emotions and cognitions in self consistency. In D. J. Bearisson and H. Zimiles (eds): Thought and Emotion; Developmental Perspectives. Hillsdale, NJ: Erlbaum.

Broughton, J. (1978) The cognitive developmental approach to morality: A reply to Kurtines and Greif. *Journal of Moral Education*, 7:81-96.

Brown, L., Argyris, D., Attanucci, J., Bardoge, B., Gilligan, C., Johnston, K., Miller, B., Osborne, D., Ward, J., Wiggins, G., and

Wilcox, D. (1987) A guide to reading narratives of moral conflict and choice for self and moral orientation. GEHD Study Center, Harvard University Graduate School of Education.

Brown, R., and Herrnstein, R. J. (1975) Psychology. Boston: Little, Brown.

Candee, D. (1976) Structure and choice in moral reasoning. *Journal of Personality and Social Psychology*, 34(6):1293–1301.

Childress, J. F. (1979) Appeals to conscience. *Ethics*, 89(4):315–335.

Childress, J. F. (1982) Moral Responsibility in Conflict. Baton Rouge: Louisiana State University.

Cohen, C. (1968) Conscientious objection. *Ethics*, lxxviii:269–279.

Cohen, C. (1971) Civil Disobedience: Conscience, Tactics and the Law. New York: Columbia University Press.

Colby, A., Kohlberg, L., Gibbs, J., Speicher, Dubin B., Candee, D., Hewer, A., and Power, C. (1987) The measurement of moral judgement: Standard issue scoring manual, vol. 2. New York: Cambridge University Press.

Curry, D. G. (1985) Sunshine patriots — punishment and the Vietnam offender. South Bend, IN: University of Notre Dame Press.

Damon, W. (1980) Structural developmental theory and the study of moral development. In M. Windmiller, N. Lambert, and E. Turiel (eds): Moral Development and Socialization (pp. 35–68). Boston: Allyn and Bacon.

Damon, W. (1983) Social and Personality Development: From Infancy through Adolescence. New York: Norton.

Durant, W., and Durant, A. (1968) The Lessons of History. New York: Simon and Schuster.

Dupuy, T. N., and Martell, P. (1985) Flawed Victory — The 1982 War in Lebanon. Fairfax, VA: Hero Books.

Eisenberg-Berg, N. (1979) Development of children's prosocial moral judgement. *Developmental Psychology*, 15(2):128–147.

Emler, N. (1983) Morality and politics: The ideological dimension in the theory of moral development. In H. Weinrich Haste and D. Locke (eds): Morality in the Making — Thoughts Action and Social Context (pp. 47–70). Chichester: Wiley.

Emler, N., Renwick, S., and Malone, B. (1983) The relationship between moral reasoning and political orientation. *Journal of Personality and Social Psychology*, 45(3):1073–1080.

Erikson, E. H. (1970) Gandhi's Truth — on the Origins of Militant Nonviolence. London: Faber and Faber.

Frankl, V. E. (1966) The Doctor and the Soul: From Psychotherapy to Logotherapy. New York: Knopf.

Feeney, T. J. (1987) Expert psychological testimony on credibility issues. *Military Law Review*, 115:121–177.

Fromm, E. (1982) On Disobedience — and Other Essays. New York: Seabury Press.

Gabison, R. (1986) The crime of the blue-white collar. *Politic*, (April 7): 28–30.

Gabriel, R. (1984) Operation Peace for the Galilee: The Israeli-PLO War in Lebanon. New York: Hill and Wang.

Gabriel, R. A., and Savage, P. L. (1981) Crisis in the Command. (Hebrew) Israel: Ministry of Defense, publishing offices.

Gal, R. (1985) Commitment and obedience in the military: An Israeli case study. *Armed Forces and Society*, 11(4):553–564.

Gal, R. (1986) A Portrait of the Israeli Soldier. Westport, CT: Greenwood Press.

Gaylin, W. (1970) In the Service of Their Country: War Resisters in Prison. New York: Grosset and Dunlap.

Gibbs, J. C. (1978) Kohlberg's stages of moral development: A constructive critique. *Harvard Educational Review*, 13:33–44.

Gibbs, J. C., Widaman, K. F., and Colby, A. (1982) Construction and validation of a simplified group administerable equivalent to the moral judgment interview. *Child Development*, 53:895–910.

Gilligan, C. (1982a) In a Different Voice. Cambridge, MA: Harvard University Press.

Gilligan, C. (1982b) New maps of development: New visions of maturity. *American Journal of Orthopsychiatry*, 52(2):199–212.

Gilligan, C. (1986) Remapping the moral domain: New Images of the self in relationship. In Thomas C. Heller, Morton Sosna, and David E. Wellbery (eds): Reconstructing Individualism: Autonomy, Individuality and the Self in the Western Thought. Palo Alto: Stanford University Press.

Gilligan, C. and Attanucci, J. (1988) Two Moral Orientations: Implications for Developmental Theory and Assessment. Merril Palmer Quarterly, 34, 3, 223–237.

Gilligan, C., and Murphy, J. M. (1979) Development from adolescence to adulthood: The philosopher and the "dilemma of the fact." In D. Kuhn (ed): Intellectual Development beyond Childhood. New Directions in Child Development (pp. 85–99). San Francisco: Jossey-Bass.

Gilligan, C., and Wiggins, G. (1987) The origins of morality in early childhood relationships. In J. Kagan and S. Lamb (eds): The Emergence of Morality in Young Children. Chicago: University of Chicago Press.

Glazer, P., and Glazer, M. (1977) War resisters in the Land of Battles. *Dissent*, 24:289–296.

Goffman, E. (1959) The Presentation of Self in Every Day Life. New York: Doubleday.

Greenberg, D. S. (1983) Health care in Israel. *New England Journal of Medicine*, 309:181–184.

Haan, N. (1975) Hypothetical and actual moral reasoning in a situation of civil disobedience. *Journal of Personality and Social Psychology*, 32: 255–269.

Haan, N., Smith, B., and Block, J. (1968) The moral reasoning of young adults. *Journal of Personality and Social Psychology*, 10:183–201.

Hardan, D. (ed) (1985) The Moral and Existential Dilemmas of the Israeli Soldier. Jerusalem: World Zionist Organisation, Center for Programming, Department of Development.

Hare, R. M. (1981) Moral Thinking—Its Levels, Method and Point. Oxford: Oxford University Press.

Hersh, S. M. (1970) My Lai 4—A Report on the Massacre and Its Aftermath. New York: Random House.

Hoffman, S. (1981) Duties beyond Borders: On the Limits and Possibilities of Ethical International Politics. Syracuse, NY: Syracuse University Press.

Hogan, R., Johnson, J. A., and Emler, N. P. (1977) A socioanalytic theory of moral development. In W. Damon (ed): The Social World of the Child. San Francisco: Jossey-Bass.

Jenkins, B. M. (1986) Statement about terrorism. In S. Anzovin (ed): Terrorism (pp. 7–18). New York: H. W. Wilson.

Katriel, T. (1986) Talking Straight: "Dugree" Speech in Israeli Sabra Culture. New York: Cambridge Press.

Kohlberg, L. (1958) The development of modes of moral thinking and choice in the years of ten to sixteen. Unpublished Ph.D. dissertation, University of Chicago.

Kohlberg, L. (1969) Stages and sequence: The cognitive developmental approach to socialization. In D. A. Goslin (ed): Handbook of Socialization Theory and Research. Chicago: Rand McNally.

Kohlberg, L. (1970) Education for justice: A modern statement of the platonic view. In N. F. Sizer (ed): Moral Education: Five Lectures. Boston: Harvard University Press.

Kohlberg, L. (1971) From is to ought: How to commit the naturalistic fallacy and get away with it in the study of moral development. In T. Mischel (ed): Cognitive Development and Genetic Epistemology (pp. 151–235). New York: Academic Press.

Kohlberg, L. (1976) Moral stages and moralization: The cognitive developmental approach. In T. Lickona (ed): Moral Development and Behavior: Theory, Research and Social Issues (pp. 31–53). New York: Holt.

Kohlberg, L. (1980) Meaning and measurement of moral development. Heinz Werner Lecture. Worcester, MA: Clark University Press.

Kohlberg, L. (1981) Essays on Moral Development, Vol 1: The Philosophy of Moral Development. San Francisco: Harper and Row.

Kohlberg, L. (1984) The Psychology of Moral Development. San Francisco: Harper and Row.

Kohlberg, L., and Candee, D. (1984) The relationship of moral judgement to moral action. In W. Kurtines and J. Gewirtz (eds): Morality, Moral Behavior and Moral Development (pp. 52–73). New York: Wiley International.

King, M. Jr. (1964) Why We Can't Wait. New York: Harper and Row.

Krebs, D., and Rosenwald, A. (1977) Moral reasoning and moral behavior in conventional adults. Merril Palmer Quarterly, 23:79–84.

Krebs, R. L. (1967) Some relationships between moral judgement, attention and resistance to temptation. Unpublished doctoral dissertation, University of Chicago, 1967.

Krebs, R., and Kohlberg, L. (1973) Moral judgement and ego controls as determinants of resistance to cheating. Cambridge: Center for Moral Education, Harvard University, 1973, mimeo.

Langer, T. (1969) Theories of Development. New York: Holt.

Laqueur, W. (1977) Terrorism. Boston: Little, Brown.

Leibowitz, N. (1976) Studies in Shemot. The Book of Exodus. Jerusalem: The World Education and Culture in the Diaspora.

Lickona, T. (1980) What does moral psychology have to say? In B. Callahan (ed): Ethics Teaching in Higher Education (pp. 103–132). New York: Plenum Press.

Linn, R. (1985) The moral judgement of the Lebanon war refusers. Studies in Education, November, 43, 19–32 (Hebrew).

Linn, R. (1986) Conscientious objection in Israel during the war in Lebanon. *Armed Forces and Society*, 12(4):489–511.

Linn, R. (1987a) Moral disobedience during the Lebanon War: What can the cognitive–developmental approach learn from the experience of the Israeli soldiers? *Social Cognition*, 5(4):383–402.

Linn, R. (1987b) Moral reasoning and behavior of striking physicians in Israel. *Psychological Reports*, 60:443–453.

Linn, R. (1988) Moral judgement in extreme social contexts—what can be learned from the experience of soldiers who refuse to fight during war and physicians who refuse to provide medical care during strike? *Journal of Applied Social Psychology*, 18, 13, 1149–1170.

Linn, R. (1988a) Terrorism, morality and soldiers' motivation to fight: An example from the war in Lebanon. *Terrorism: An International Journal*, 11, 139–149.

Linn, R. (1989a) Hypothetical and actual moral reasoning of Israeli selective conscientious objectors during the war in Lebanon (1982–1985). *Journal of Applied Developmental Psychology*, 10(1), 19–36.

Linn, R. (1989b) The moral judgement, action and credibility of Israeli reserve soldiers who refused to serve in Lebanon. In M. Noone (ed): Selective Conscientious Objectors — Problems and Prospects. West View Press, CO.

Linn, R. The power to act morally — Refusers and Peace Now activists discuss their moral integrity (in preparation).

Linn, R., and Gilligan, C. (1989) One action two moral orientations: The emergence of justice and care voices among selective conscientious objectors. *New Ideas in Psychology* 7(3).

Locke, D. (1981) Cognitive stage or developmental phases? A critique of Kohlberg's stage structural theory of moral reasoning. *Journal of Moral Education*, 8(3):168–181.

Locke, D. (1983a) Doing what comes morally. *Human Development*, 26:11–25.

Locke, D. (1983b). Theory and practice in thought and action. In Weinrich-Haste, H., and Locke, D. (eds): Morality in the Making — Thoughts Action and Social Context (pp. 157–170). Chichester: Wiley.

Loevinger, J. (1976) Ego Development. San Francisco: Jossey-Bass.

Luttwak, E., and Horowitz, D. (1983) The Israeli Army, 1948–1973. Cambridge, MA: ABT Books.

Lyons, N. (1982) Conceptions of self and morality and modes of moral choice. Unpublished doctoral dissertation, Harvard University. 1982.

McNamee, S. (1978). Moral behavior, moral development and motivation. *Journal of Moral Education*, 7:27–31.

Marshal, S. L. A. (1978) Men against Fire. Gloucester, MA: Peter Smith.

Melzer, Y. (1975) Concepts of Just War. Leyden, Holland: Sijhoff.

Merari, A. (1985) On Terrorism and Combating Terrorism. University Publications of America, Inc.

Milgram, S. (1974) Obedience to Authority. New York: Harper and Row.

Mosher, R. (1980) Moral Education: A First Generation of Research and Development. New York: Praeger.

Murphy, J. M., and Gilligan, C. (1980) Moral development in late adolescence and adulthood: As critic and reconstruction of Kohlberg's theory. *Human Development*, 23:77–104.

Netanyahu, B. (1986) Terrorism, How the West Can Win. New York: Farrar, Straus and Giroux.

O'Brien, W. V. (1986) Terrorism — What should we do? In S. Anzovin (ed): Terrorism (pp. 153–159). New York: H. W. Wilson.

Orwell, G. (1949) 1984. New York: Harcourt, Brace and World.

Pearl, C. (ed): (1970) Rashi — Commentaries on the Pentatuch. New York: Norton.

Peri, Y. (1983) The rise and the fall of Israel's national consensus. *New Outlook*, August–September, 28–29.

Phillips, R. L. (1984) War and Justice. Norman: University of Oklahoma Press.

Piaget, J. (1932/1965) The Moral Judgement of the Child. New York: New Press.

Rapoport, D. C. (1984) Fear and trembling: terrorism in three religious traditions. *American Political Science Review*, 38(3):658–677.

Sandler, T., Tshirrhart, J. T., and Cauley, J. A. (1983) Theoretical analysis of transitional terrorism. *American Political Science Review*, 77:36–54.

Sarna, N. M. (1966) Understanding Genesis. New York: McGraw-Hill.

Scheissel, L. (1968) Conscience in America. New York: Dutton.

Schiff, Z., and Yaari, E. (1984) Israel's Lebanon War (trans and ed Ina Friedman). New York: Simon and Schuster.

Schuman, H. (1972) Two sources of antiwar sentiment in America. *American Journal of Sociology*, 78(3):513–536.

Shapira, A. (ed): (1971) The Seventh Day — Soldiers Talk about the Six Day War. New York: Penguin Books.

Shiffer, S. (1984) Snow Ball — The Story behind the Lebanon War. Yediot Acharonot Books, Edanim Publishers (Hebrew).

Sichel, B. A. (1985) Women's moral development in search of philosophical assumptions. *Journal of Moral Education*, 14(3):149–160.

Sick, G. G. (1987) Terrorism: Its political use and abuse. SAIS (School of advanced international studies), Johns Hopkins University, 7(1).

Siegler, M. (1982) Decision making strategy or clinical-ethical problems in medicine. *Archive of Internal Medicine*, 142:2178–2179.

Slotowitz, M. (1977) Genesis — A new translation with a commentary anthologized from Talmudic Midrashic and Rabbinic sources. Morasha Publication.

Snarey, J. R., Reimer, J., and Kohlberg, L. (1985) Development of social-moral reasoning among Kibbutz adolescent: A longitudinal cross cultural study. *Developmental Psychology*, 21(1):3–17.

Sprinzak, E. (1977) Extreme politics in Israel. *The Jerusalem Quarterly*, 5: 33–47.

Tilling, L. (1972) Sincerity and Authenticity. Cambridge, MA: Harvard University Press.

Timmerman, J. (1985) The Longest War: Israel in Lebanon. New York: Knopf.

Walzer, M. (1968) Civil disobedience and "resistance." *Dissent,* Jan–Feb 13–15.

Walzer, M. (1977) Just and Unjust Wars. New York: Basic Books.

Walzer, M. (1970) Obligations; Essays on Disobedience, War and Citizenship. Cambridge: Harvard University Press.

Weinrich-Haste, H., and Locke, D. (1983) Morality in the making: Thoughts action and the social context. Chichester: Wiley.

Zashin, E. (1972) M. Civil Disobedience and Democracy. New York: Free Press.

NEWSPAPERS

Ma'ariv, May 2, 1988.

Ha'aretz, October 10, 1984.

Israel TV, April 30, 1985.

Ha'ir, April 22, 1983.

Ha'aretz, March 11, 1983.

Jerusalem Post, August 2, 1982.

Jerusalem Post, September 17, 1982.

Jerusalem Post, May 17, 1983.

Jerusalem Post, May 24, 1982.

New York Times Magazine, October 30, 1983.

Ha'ir, July 9, 1982.

Ha'ir, April 22, 1983.

Yediot Acharonot, August 14, 1987.

Ha'aretz, April 11, 1985.

Ha'aretz, August 10, 1984.

Ha'aretz, September 23, 1983.

Yediot Acharonot, December 28, 1984.

Ma'ariv, May 17, 1984.

Ha'aretz, June 7, 1985.

Ma'ariv, June 7, 1985.

Yediot Acharonot, June 7, 1985.

Appendices

APPENDIX 1: KOHLBERG'S FORM B TEST (1984)

There was a woman who had very bad cancer, and there was no treatment known to medicine that would save her. Her doctor, Dr. Jefferson, knew that she had only about six months to live. She was in terrible pain, but she was so weak that a good dose of pain killer like morphine would make her die sooner. She was delirious and almost crazy with pain and in her calm periods she would ask Dr. Jefferson to give her enough morphine to kill her. She said she could not stand the pain and she was going to die in a few months anyway. Although he knows that mercy killing is against the law, the doctor thinks about granting her request.

1. Should Dr. Jefferson give her the drug that would make her die? 1a. Why or why not?
2. Is it actually right or wrong for him to give the woman the drug that would make her die? 2a. Why is it right or wrong?
3. Should the woman have the right to make the final decision? 3a. Why is it right or wrong?
4. The woman is married. Should the husband have anything to do with the decision? 4a. Why or why not?
5. It is against the law for the doctor to give the woman the drug. Does that make it morally wrong? 5a. Why or why not?
6. In general, should people try to do everything they can to obey the

law? 6a. Why or why not? 6b. How does this apply to what Dr. Jefferson should do?

Dr. Jefferson did perform the mercy killing by giving the woman the drug. Passing by at the time was another doctor, Dr. Rogers, who knew the situation Dr. Jefferson was in. Dr. Rogers thought of trying to stop Dr. Jefferson, but the drug was already administered. Dr. Rogers wonders whether he should report Dr. Jefferson.

1. Should Dr. Rogers report Dr. Jefferson? 1a. Why or why not?

Dr. Rogers did report Dr. Jefferson. Dr. Jefferson is brought to court and a jury is selected. It is up to the judge to determine the sentence.

2. Should the judge give Dr. Jefferson some sentence, or should he suspend the sentence and let Dr. Jefferson go free? 2a. Why is that best?
3. Thinking in terms of society, should people who break the law be punished? 3a. Why or why not? 3b. How does this apply to how they should decide?
4. Dr. Jefferson was doing what his conscience told him when he gave the woman the drug. Should a law breaker be punished if he is acting out of conscience? 4a. Why? (Kohlberg 1984, 644–645).

Note: The description of the jury's role in the trial of Dr. Jefferson was omitted in order to match the dilemma to the Israeli experience. The same was done in regard to the question of the death penalty.

APPENDIX 2: THE ACTUAL MORAL REASONING INTERVIEW

1. How did the idea of refusal come to your mind?
2. When did you refuse? Why? Why did you not refuse on the first day of the war?
3. How and why did refusal become a concrete alternative for you?
4. Why do you think refusal is/was the right action? How do you justify it?
5. Why was it right for you to take the law into your own hands?
6. Do you regard this action as a responsible one? Why?

7. Did you convince other friends to refuse? Why?

8. Is it right for a soldier who has been called to evacuate citizens from a settlement in the occupied territories to refuse? Why?

9. At what point do you think that a soldier has the right to refuse the army's command? Why?

10. What "price" were you willing to pay for the refusal? Why?

11. What role does fear play in your decision to refuse? Why?

12. To what extent does this action match your own and others' expectations?

13. Did you know other refusers? What did you think about the motives of the other refusers? Why?

14. What was the final straw in your decision-making process? Why?

15. What was the hardest part in this decision-making process?

16. What were the specific factors that helped you in the decision-making process? In the construction of the action? To cope with the consequences of the action?

17. Was the punishment you received justified? Why?

18. What did you tell yourself after serving your term in prison? Why?

19. What did you expect to be the impact of your action? Why?

20. How do you envision your future? Why?

21. Would you refuse again when your unit is called again? Why?

22. Is there any other question that you would suggest I ask refusers like yourself that I have not asked?

APPENDIX 3: SCORING GUIDE FOR ACTUAL MORAL REASONING IN SUPPORT OF REFUSAL (BASED ON KOHLBERG'S 1983 SCORING MANUAL)

Transitional Stage 2/3

Ambiguous reference to the refuser's motives for action.

A. *Critical Indicators:* Required for a match are both (a) Some reference to the refuser's lack of bad intentions (all that I could do is to refuse. . . . I was not hurting anybody by refusing . . .), and (b) some reference to helping others by taking the action (I would not be effective anyhow — they would be better without me).

I think I am the one who knows best what is good for myself. I could never before envision myself as a refuser. I was always a dedicated soldier. I do not think that it is my fault that I refuse now because there was no other option for action for me . . . at least the only way I could solve my own problem with the war was to refuse . . . at least I do not fight anybody, if my friends want to die in the war they can — I do not stand in their way . . . it is easier for me to be punished than to go to war though I am not sure that such an action, which is a response to a situation that I did not create, should be punished.

Stage 3

Refusal is performed out of good intention. It might be right or wrong — however good the motives of the actor. Because the government/army were not considering the feelings of the soldiers or the people.

A. *Critical Indicators:* Required for a match are references to both (a) a concern that the soldier should have consulted the law, other people, and (b) that if the act received some social support, then it must be right.

I have talked with friends and they were all convinced that I was really suffering from this war and that I could not function properly. Moreover, every one of them seemed to share my ideas but they could not take the stand of refusal. This general attitude of my friends gave me the feeling that I am right particularly since nobody complains that refusal to kill in this war would harm them, or that if I sit in prison they would not go.

B. *Critical Indicators:* Required for a match is a reference to either (a) the motive of refusal is empathetic (one should not sit still when so much killing is being done, etc.), and (b) direct reference to the refuser's virtuous motives (this was not a selfish action but out of concern for others.

Refusal is right because it reflects one's involvement in the situation and caring for the people involved.

C. *Critical Indicators:* Required both a match for (a) reference to refusal as a painful act for the soldier (it weighs on his conscience, etc.), and (b) need not be punished for acting out of good intentions.

Having reached the stage where you have to refuse in the IDF is a painful stage. I knew it was wrong to refuse but I had no choice since as a soldier, this is the only means I have. I guess those who do not consider refusal in the IDF do not know what we are going through — it is not a simple decision to do the opposite of what your friends are doing though you love your country like they do. I do not say that they do not have a conscience too, but maybe it is easier for them to go. My commander knew it was not an easy decision for me, and I am surprised that he thought that I should be punished although I was sincere.

Transitional Stage 3/4

Refusal is performed out of good conscience. Focus on the careful and deliberate way in which the soldier made the decision to refuse, or his attempt to behave in accordance with his own conscience. Emphasis on the soldier's role obligations in terms of specific duties he has sworn to carry out. Begins to understand morality in terms of internal moral standards.

A. *Critical Indicators:* Required for a match are both aspects of the appeal to (a) promoting or setting an example or (b) prosocial motives (compassion, concern, caring, etc.).

I refused in order to set an example for my friends in order to take them out of their apathetic stage. They could watch the TV, hear about these killings and go to the reserve service the next day. This was the only way I could encourage my commander and friends to stop their routine and say to themselves: Just a moment what is he doing? If he is not joining us, something must be wrong here.

B. *Critical Indicators:* Required for a match are either (a) the suggestion that refusal was right in the soldier's own mind (he did what he thought was right, made the best decision he could, etc.) because (b) he had considered the decision carefully (he had thought about both sides of this difficult decision, he had looked at it from different points of view, he had thought about it for a long time, etc.), or (c) the suggestion that breaking the law out of concern for others (to end the war) could have been justifiable from the soldier's perspective.

I had two options, either to go with everybody and to lie and betray my beliefs, or to refuse, which I felt was the more appropriate action for me since in this way I do not give my hand to these killings. As a dedicated soldier, it was a very hard decision to make, but taking this stand and even breaking the law was the only right response I could make. I am sure that my action of refusal is important to the unit as well as my former obedient behavior. It is not a spur of the moment decision — I have invested a lot of thought about it and examined this decision from all sides. It was quite painful but I am glad I could act in line with my convictions — at least I hope that this is what my kids will learn from me.

C. *Critical Indicators:* Required for a match are both (a) some explicit statement that the soldier's intent modifies the severity of refusal within the IDF and (b) a judgment that the severity of the punishment should match the severity of this action.

The Lebanon War is not a typical war that the Israeli soldiers are trained to fight. This was a different war — if you look around you see that there is no consensus about it. I believe that some people do not break the law simply because they are indifferent . . . in this war, there was a feeling of dying in vain, and how should one expect obedience to the law in such a case . . . I am sure that my commander would have refused if he was in my place. I guess my commander realized that I am not a law breaker per se and that is why he did not give me the full punishment he could have.

Stage 4

Refusal is an action which is performed by a conscientious and responsible person/citizen who has contributed much to society. Refusal is instrumental to the pursuit of social values and goals of the IDF and Israeli society at large. Attention to the formal limitations of a rule-based legal system. A differentiation of moral law from civil or legal law and an appreciation of the greater validity of the former. The policy of the war should be examined in moral terms.

A. *Critical Indicators:* Required for a match is reference to either (a) the soldier's character in terms of "good citizen, member of society," conscientious, responsible, etc., or (b) contributions the soldier has made to society (has acted in society's best interests, etc.).

I guess it is my role as an Israeli citizen to defend my country not only as a fighting soldier, but also as a citizen who cares for the norms of his society . . . and when I feel that these norms are being violated, at least in this war—I should protest. It is not only good for me, it is for the best for Israeli society at large where unfortunately wars are so frequent.

B. *Critical Indicators:* Required for a match are both (a) the idea of moral law or dictates of conscience and (b) a suggestion that going by one's moral law is at least as important to society as civil law. Focus on the soldier's past contributions to society (or his act in the best interests of society as an indication of his status as a good or conscientious citizen).

I have always been an obedient citizen in terms of my army's obligation— unlike many of my friends who employed various excuses in order to evade service. . . . In a vulnerable country such as Israel, service in the army is an important obligation and if you refuse to do it, as I did this time, you should be aware that you are breaking one of the most important societal rules. However, I believe that as a member of this society—I have contributed more to the entire society by bringing its attention to the limitations of this rule in the case of the futility of this war rather than harming society.

C. *Critical Indicators:* Required for a match are both aspects of a suggestion that (a) the law cannot justify application or should not in fairness be applied to all cases because (b) it is unsuitable for every case or circumstance.

The command to serve in Lebanon is not illegal and therefore, theoretically, I am not obliged to refuse. However, this command does not account for all the immoral issues that I would face there—the issue of life and death is more important for me and ought to guide my action more than the law.

Transitional Stage 4/5

The right to refuse should be provided by the state. The focus is on state rights as limited to those rights according to individuals. A state should not dictate anything that is wrong for the individuals in that society. There is a recognition that some of the blame or responsibility must be attributed to society and that part of the commitment one makes in remaining a member of that society is to accept the burdens that are associated with this responsibility.

A. *Critical Indicators:* Required for a match is reference to either (a) the subjective nature of moral refusal, role interpretations, etc., or (b) the importance of respecting or the legitimacy of refusal and interpretations made by others.

For me, refusal is the right action since it falls within the scope of any legitimate interpretation of a soldier's definite role and particularly within the framework of the ethical guidelines of the IDF as *tohar haneshek*.

B. *Critical Indicators:* Required for a match are both (a) an idea that law or legal sentencing should reflect justice, and (b) a suggestion that the judging commander can or should relate law to justice in his sentencing (can find a precedent, develop a rule, etc.).

I think that the IDF should provide us with the right to refuse and not only with the right to kill . . . The war in Lebanon is a precedent since it is not a purely defensive war.

C. *Critical Indicators:* Required for a match are both (a) a distinction between the soldier's moral point of view and a social or legal point of view of what is right, and (b) an implicit suggestion that the point of view adopted is a personal or subjective matter.

Under the immoral circumstances of the Lebanon War, refusal is justified because the soldier, though obliged to kill, should act in line with his moral judgement in any case and live with his conscience or punishment as a result of his own action. Israeli society or the IDF should be secondary in this case.

Stage 5

The individual has the right not to kill. This is a "prior to society" human right. Rights are conceptualized as including the right to liberty, limited only in regard to the rights of others. Moral law can be defined as the protection of human rights, and this protection of rights constitutes the underlying purpose of the legal system itself. The collective good or social welfare reduces to the welfare and protection of rights of each individual in the society.

A. *Critical Indicators:* Required for a match is reference to either of the following: (a) the limits of freedom, autonomy, or individual rights as deriving from or defined by potential conflict between individuals who are seeking to exercise those rights, or (b) some formal mechanism designed to impartially protect rights to both life and autonomy from irrationality or irresponsibility of the government or the army or the society at large.

The act of refusal is not in conflict with the others' right to go and fight . . . I guess what the individual soldier decides to do with his own life is his right and his responsibility . . . My decision to refuse has been made in the most objective way and has been acknowledged as rational even by people who are involved in the war or those who hold a different position in Israel society (a third party).

B. *Critical Indicators:* Required for a match is a reference to either (a) the act of refusal is an affirmation of the soldier's right to life, autonomy, etc., (b) the law that does not allow conscientious refusal is wrong as it conflicts with human rights, or (c) the function or the purpose of the law as the protection of human rights.

Indeed, by refusing to go to Lebanon I broke the law. But I do not consider this law as a good one since it conflicts with my right not to kill (or be killed by) another human being that is more important to me than the law. The right to live is not only mine. It also belongs to the people across the border. In this case, I do not care about the IDF concerns.

C. *Critical Indicators:* Required for a match are references to both (a) a distinction between individual rights or welfare and social welfare (collective good, benefits to the group), and (b) individual rights, welfare, etc., as more basic than the welfare of society as a whole (collective good has no meaning beyond the sum of the welfare of individuals).

I am not worried that the IDF would be weakened because of my refusal. It is a sign of moral strength of any army if its soldiers have the right to express moral concerns. I think the IDF is weakened if nobody has the right to refuse. What is the meaning of the idea that the war is going to protect our right to exist when the individual's right (the one who makes the society) is not respected? I do not advocate refusal per se, and each case should be carefully examined but the main point is that the soldier's right to refuse comes before society.

Index

About the Author

RUTH LINN, who served on the Israel Defense Forces from 1968 to 1970, is now in the Department of Education at the University of Haifa in Haifa, Israel.